ULSTER

A Story of Warfare and Conquest in Ancient Ireland

Michael Sheane

ARTHUR H. STOCKWELL LTD
Torrs Park   Ilfracombe   Devon
Established 1898
www.ahstockwell.co.uk

British Library Cataloguing-in-Publication Data.
A catalogue record for this book is available
from the British Library.

By the same author:
Ulster & Its Future After the Troubles (1977)
Ulster & The German Solution (1978)
Ulster & The British Connection (1979)
Ulster & The Lords of the North (1980)
Ulster & The Middle Ages (1982)
Ulster & St Patrick (1984)
The Twilight Pagans (1990)
Enemy of England (1991)
The Great Siege (2002)
Ulster in the Age of Saint Comgall of Bangor (2004)
Ulster Blood (2005)
King William's Victory (2006)
Ulster Stock (2007)
Famine in the Land of Ulster (2008)
Pre-Christian Ulster (2009)
The Glens of Antrim (2010)
Ulster Women – A Short History (2010)

ISBN 978-0-7223-4061-5
Printed in Great Britain by
Arthur H. Stockwell Ltd
Torrs Park   Ilfracombe
Devon

Contents

Introduction

There is a dearth of early literature on Ireland. Much of what remains is derived from the Middle Ages. Four groups of stories have been handed down to us:

1) Mythological stories relating to the Tuatha Dé Danann (The Tribes of the Goddess Danu), an ancient divine race said to have inhabited the island of Ireland before the time of the Celts.
2) The Ulster Cycle, which deals with the exploits of King Conchobor and the champions of the Red Branch Knights of Emain Macha (Armagh), whose chief was Cúchulainn, the Hound of Ulster.
3) The Fenian Cycle, which deals with the exploits of Finn MacCool, his son Oisín and the other warriors of the fianna.
4) A group of stories centred upon various kings, said to have reigned between the third century BC and the eighth century AD.

The oldest of the early manuscripts is *Lebor na hUidre,* commonly know as the *Book of the Dun Cow*.

It was transcribed at the monastery of Clonmacnoise in the twelfth century. It contains in a badly flawed and mutilated text part of the earliest known manuscript of the Táin Bó Cúailnge. There is also *The Yellow Book of Lecan,* a fourteenth-century manuscript.

The origins of the Táin Bó Cúailnge are much more ancient than these manuscripts. The language of the earliest part of the story dates to the eighth century, but the verse passages may be two centuries older. It is held by most Celtic scholars that the Ulster Cycle existed at the time of Christ. This idea is supported by the barbaric world of the tales, uninfluenced by classical scholars. The Táin and certain descriptions of Gaulish society by classical authors have many details in common, such as the many weapons, the boastfulness of warriors, and the practices of cattle-raiding, chariot-fighting and beheading. Ireland was isolated and could retain traits and customs that had disappeared elsewhere centuries before. It is possible that the type of culture the Táin describes may have lasted in Ireland up to the coming of Christianity in the fifth century. The Táin itself, considered as a unit, lacks a number of important elements: the motive for the Connaught invasion of Ulster, the reason for the sickness of the Ulster warriors throughout most of the action, the reasons for Fergus's opposition to Conchobor and the reasons for the presence of a troop of Ulster exiles in the Connaught forces. All these elements must be considered.

There are other tales, and many remscéla, or pre-tales, leading up to the Táin. Though not strictly part of the story, they are important as they give information about the lives of the kings and heroes of the Ulster Cycle.

The first section of the Cycle consists of a group or pre-tales important for their understanding of the plot and motivations of the Táin. Their source can be identified in the tales. A separate series, identified in the tales, deals with the building-up of allies for war on Ulster and the arrangements for provisioning their forces. The excuse for invasion is supplied in *The Book of Leinster,* another major manuscript.

The language of *The Book of Leinster* version of the Táin can be dated to the twelfth century, and the tale survives complete.

The author of the book took pains to provide a consistent narrative. Perhaps because of its completeness *The Book of Leinster* Táin has attracted considerable attention from editors and translators. There is an abridged version by Standish Hayes O'Grady in Eleanor Hull's *The Cuchullin Saga,* published in 1898. It had a German translation by Ernst Windisch in 1905. Other versions followed. The Dublin Institute of Advanced Studies published a new edition in 1967 with an English translation by Cecile O'Rahilly. Of the earlier versions only one has been published, by Winifred Faraday in 1904, but it is incomplete and difficult to read. These might be grounds for choosing the *Lebor na hUidre* or *The Yellow Book of Lecan* for a new translation. The complier of *The Book of Leinster* had, besides a care for completeness, a generally florid and adjectival style, falling at times to decadence.

The early texts in *The Book of Leinster* are the work of many hands and in places it is little more than the mangled remains of many scribes. There are significant inconsistencies and repetitions of incidents. Sometimes the narrative withers away into obscure notes and summaries. Extraneous matter has been added, varying from complete glosses to additions from other sources. Frank O'Connor in *The Backward Look,* incorporates his short history of Irish literature, wherein a cattle raid has been rendered almost unintelligible. However, many of the mistakes can be remedied, and a reasonably readable narrative produced. Modern translations of the Táin have simplified matters. The story has been freed from inconsistencies and repetitions, and obscure passages have been made simple (generally from the text given in *The Book of Leinster*). This editing has been done as sparingly as possible; alteration has been kept to a minimum. Some passages have been inserted by the compiler for the sake of clarity, and they can be recognized by the change in style.

Two aspects of the translation have not been fully covered. The first has to do with the main purpose of the work, which was to provide a vivid account of affairs. Sentence structure and tenses have been altered without hesitation; elements are occasionally shifted from one sentence to another. Different verbs have been used. The second aspect has to do with the verse passages. There is more freedom with the verse than with the prose, though the sense is maintained.

Passages of *rosc* or *retiorice* occur throughout the translation, and in the original these are extremely obscure. This is partly because they are archaic, but it seems likely that in some cases, where the note is prophetic, the obscurity is also deliberate. Scholars have tended to leave these verses unaltered, but it seems worthwhile to make some sense out of them, especially where something very relevant to the action is taking place. The object has been to produce passages of verse which more or less match the original for length, ambiguity and obscurity. Occasionally there are short runs that cannot be understood in the Irish. It would not have been possible to attack these passages without expert help. Dr Mac Cana of University College Dublin has suggested that they provide a starting point for the imagination, and they underwent much alteration, for which the translator is entirely responsible. There has been no attempt to follow the Irish verses.

For a proper consideration of the Táin in Irish literature, a list of further reading is listed in the bibliography, and there are comments on historical, mythological, symbolic, and other important aspects. Scholars and commentators continue to pursue these topics with remarkable results – Alwyn and Brinley Rees, for example. In their *Celtic Heritage*, the Táin appears as an example of the classic struggle between the priests and the warrior class, each of which seems to contradict the function of the other. Heinrich Zimmer saw the pillow talk that gave rise to the Táin as a fight between Celtic-Aryan father-dominance and the mother-dominance of the pre-Celtic inhabitants of the British Isles. Frank O'Connor has suggested that the earlier layers of the tale, not well preserved in the *rosc* passages, constitute the remains of an ironic anti-feminist poem. T. F. O'Rahilly believes that the Ulster tales, recording the Ui Neill invaders from Leinster (not Connaught), were the brainchild of Maeve, Queen of Connaught. She is called Medb by some authors, and she is associated with the goddess Memair, of Tara, in Leinster. This appears to be a mistake, for the Irish tribes did not have queens.

A few features of the Táin as it is presented here seem to call for explanation. It is evident that, even allowing for the later interpolations, there is no overall narrative tone. The story is told in some places with great realism, and in others with an air of folk history or fantasy. It is also evident that the verbal quality of the story was valued more than consistency. Finnabair, who died of shame, was brought back to life at the end of the Táin and resided with Cúchulainn, but this is inconsistent with the account at the end of 'Cúchulainn's Courtship of Emer'. Lists of heroes are very likely to contain some that were dead or absent. Many were killed. Hero after hero was reluctant to meet Cúchulainn because he was a beardless youth, despite the mounting evidence of his courage. Cúchulainn vowed to kill Maeve on sight, but he forgoes his chance at the end of the Táin. He was no killer of women, it says, though he had just killed two lamenting women sent by Maeve to deceive him. Such inconsistencies are typical of epic literature; to see them as mistakes or flaws is to ignore the real nature and origin of the tales.

One of the major elements of the Táin is its topography. Place names and their fanciful meanings and origins occupy an important place. Certain incidents seem to have been invented merely to explain a place name. One outstanding example of this occurs at the conclusion of the Táin. There is a final battle, which is treated casually whilst attention is drawn to the mortally wounded brown bull, Donn Cúailnge, which wandered around Ireland, naming the places it visited.

This characteristic is not confined to the Táin, or the Ulster Cycle. It is a preoccupation of early and medieval Irish literature and occurs in a large range of works, including prose tracts and poems of great length. These poems were composed by professional poets, who were expected to recite them upon demand.

The topographical element is important for a full appreciation of the Táin. Much of the tale is taken up describing the movements of the Connaught armies across the island and back and forth over present-day County Louth in the Republic of Ireland. Some of the places in the Táin seem to have existed and in some cases the Táin place names have been replaced by English names over the years. Many names can be identified with reasonable confidence. The Táin's awareness of place names makes it possible to reconstruct maps of early Connaught and Ulster. It would have been impossible to put together these maps without expert help. This came from Professor John V. Kelleher and Gene C. Haley of Harvard University. Their findings are not always definite, but the maps help us to follow the story.

A strong point in the sagas is their directness. There are references to seduction, copulation, urination and the picking of vermin. One account describes how Cúchulainn was born. This coarseness was a matter of concern to Lady Gregory, and she left out a good deal that she did not care about for one reason or another.

Fergus's adultery with Maeve was retained, but that was only because their relationship was of importance in the saga. There is the clash with Gideon at the beginning of the expedition; there is the encounter in the wood, where Fergus clearly did not like Maeve's demands to surrender his sword, but the sword was restored before battle. Fergus vents his anger on Conchobor, the old usurper.

Perhaps the greatest achievement of the Táin and the Ulster Cycle is the presence of women, some in full scale and some in miniature. It may be as goddess figures that these women ultimately have their power, and their names stick in the memory – Maeve, Deirdre, Macha, Nes, Aife.

The story related in the Táin is continued in other sagas. 'The Battle of Ros na Ríg' tells of Ulster's war of revenge for the Táin, and of how Cúchulainn slew Coirpre, King of Temair. 'The Death of Cúroi' tells how Cúchulainn murdered Cúroi after being defeated in battle by him. 'Carnage on Murtheimne Plain' and 'The Death of Cúchulainn' tells of Ulster's defeat at the hands of her united foes, and of how Cúchulainn was killed by the sons of Coirpre, Cúroi and Calatín. Lastly, 'Conall Cernach's Red

Onslaught' tells how Conall Cernach avenged Cúchulainn's death.

These sagas, though they take the action further, do so in a very different way. There is high fantasy and a falling back upon the supernatural, so the sequels would make a very different kind of book. These stories are much inferior in quality on the whole to the Táin.

Another group of tales, amongst which are some of the best in the Ulster Cycle, deal with exploits not directly related to the Táin. The most important of these are 'Cúchulainn's Sickbed' and 'Emer's Jealously', which tell the story of the goddess Fann's love for Cúchulainn and how she lured him to the underworld. 'The Story of Mac Datho's Pig' tells of fights for supremacy amongst the Ulster peoples. 'The Courtship of Ferb' tells how Maine Morgor, a son of Maeve and Ailill, courted Gerg's daughter, and how Conchobor attacked during the wedding feast and slew Gerg and Maine and their followers.

There is also a group of 'Death Tales' of the Ulster heroes. 'The Ruin of Da Choca's Hostel' tells of the struggles for the succession after Conchobor's death, and 'Cúchulainn's Demon Chariot' tells how Cúchulainn's spirit was called up by St Patrick to help in the conversion to Christianity of Laegaire, High King of Ireland.

Chapter 1

Folklore and History

It is said that the poets of Ireland one day were gathered around Senchan Torpeist to see if any of them could remember the Táin Bó Cúailnge in its entirety. They all said they could recall only parts of it. Senchan asked which of the pupils, in return for his blessing, would journey to the land of Ketha and learn the version of the Táin that a sage took with him in exchange for the Book Cuilmenn.

Emine, Ninéne's grandson, set out for the east with Senchan's son, Muirgen. It happened that the grave of Fergus mac Róich was on their way, at Enoch in Connaught. Muirgen sat down at Fergus's gravestone, and the others left him while they looked for shelter for the night. Muirgen recited a poem at the grave, and a mist suddenly formed around him. For the space of three days and nights he could not be found. Within the mist, Fergus approached him in great majesty with a gilded sword. He had brown hair and he wore a green cloak, a red hooded tunic and bronze, blunt-toed sandals. Fergus recited to him the entire Táin from start to finish.

The news travelled back to Senchan, and he rejoiced over it. Some, however, said that the story was told by Senchan himself after he had fasted and prayed to certain saints.

Seven tales pave the way for the Táin Bó Cúailnge: 'How Conchobor was Begotten and How He Assumed the Kingship of Ulster', 'The Pangs of Ulster', 'Exile of the Sons of Uisliu', 'How Cúchulainn Was Begotten', 'Cúchulainn's Courtship of Emer and His Training in Arms with Scáthach', 'The Death of Aife's One Son', and 'The Quarrel of the Two Pig-keepers and How the Bulls Were Begotten'. Some believe that this list should also include 'Cúchulainn's Coming to the House of Culann the Smith', 'Cúchulainn's Taking Up Arms and Mounting into His Chariot' and 'Cúchulainn's Trip to Emain Macha'. These journeys, however, are mentioned in the body of the Táin.

Nes, the daughter of Eochaid of the Yellow Heel was in the company of her royal women. Cathbad, the Druid or magician from the Tratraige of Mag Inis passed by, and the girl asked him what he thought the hour was lucky for. He answered that it was lucky for conceiving a king or queen. The Queen asked if this were really true, and the Druid swore by the gods that it was. The girl saw no other man nearby, so she took him inside with her. She became heavy with child, and the child was in her womb for three years and three months. At the feast of Othar she gave birth.

The boy, Conchobor, was reared by Cathbad and was known as Cathbad's son. Conchobor rose to great importance seven years after his birth, when he became the King of Ulster. His mother, Nes had been living near by herself and Fergus mac Róich, the King of Ulster at the time, sought Nes for his wife. She agreed to sleep with him on condition that Conchobor would be proclaimed King of Ulster for a year. Fergus agreed and at once Nes set about advising her son. She arranged that one half of the population should give some of their wealth to the other half. She let the Ulster warriors have her own gold and silver.

Fergus called to ask for his kingdom back, but the men of Ulster said they would have to think about it. They were grateful to Conchobor for all he and his mother had given them. They declared that what Fergus had sold should remain sold; what Conchobor bought, let it remain so. Thus Fergus parted with the kingship of Ulster and Cathbad's son, Conchobor, became king of a province in Ireland.

The people of Ulster worshipped Conchobor. So high was their regard for him that every man that took a woman in marriage let her spend a night with Conchobor first. He never gave a judgment until it was absolutely necessary, for fear that if it was wrong, the crops would worsen. There was no braver warrior in Ireland; but because he was to produce a son, his people never let him stand in the way of danger. Heroes and warriors went before him into every contest. Any Ulsterman who gave him a bed for the night also gave him his wife to sleep with.

His household was handsome, and he had three houses: Craebruad ('the red branch'), Tete Brec ('the twinkling hoard') and Craebderg ('the ruddy branch'). Severed heads and other spoils were kept at Craebderg. The kings sat at Craebruad, red denoting royalty. All javelins, shields and swords were kept at Tete Brec. Gold and silver glistened on the warriors' necks, on the grey javelins and shields, and on the goblets, cups and drinking horns.

Conchobor's household were beyond counting. It was said that there were 150 inner rooms panelled with red yew. At the centre of the house was Conchobor's room, shielded by plates of copper, with bars of silver and gold birds. In the birds' heads precious jewels were used for eyes. Over Conchobor's head when he sat in this room was a rod of silver with three apples of gold, for keeping order over the multitude. When he shook the rod or raised his voice, everyone sank into silence so that one could hear a pin drop. At any given time in Conchobor's room thirty heroes could drink from Gerg's vat, which was always kept full.

A very rich landlord called Crunniuc mac Agnomain lived in the mountains of Ulster with all his sons. His wife was dead. One day, when he was alone in his house he saw a woman coming towards him, and she was desirable to his eyes. She settled down and started to work, as though she was well used to the house. When night fell she put everything in order without being asked, and she slept with Crunniuc. She remained with him for some time, and there was never a lack of food or clothing under her care.

After some time a fair was held in Ulster, and everyone in the kingdom was expected to attend – men and women, boys and girls. Crunniuc and his sons set out for the fair in their best clothes, but before he left home the woman said to him that it would be well not to be too boastful in anything he said. He replied that he was not likely to be.

The fair was held, and at the end of the day the King's chariots were brought on to the field. The crowd cried that nothing could beat those horses, but Crunniuc said his wife was faster. He was immediately taken before the King, and the woman was sent for. She told the messenger that it would be a heavy burden for her to go with him and run against the horses for she was full with child. The messenger said he would die unless she came. She was not in a good mood, and when she arrived at the fair she called out to the crowd that they must wait until the child was born, but she could not move them. She said much evil would flow from this. The King asked her her name, and she said she was Macha, daughter of Sainrith mac Imbaith.

She raced the chariot, and as she reached the end of the field she gave birth to twins, a son and a daughter. The name Emain Macha ('the twins of Macha') derives from this. As she gave birth, she screamed out in pain and suffered for five days and four nights. This same affliction seized all the men of Ulster who were present that day and nine generations after them. For nine generations any Ulsterman suffering those pangs had no more strength than a woman on the bed of labour. Only three groups of people were free from the pangs: the young boys of the kingdom, the women and Cúchulainn. Ulster was thus afflicted from the time of Crunniuc, the son of Agnomain, son of Curir Ulad, son of Fiatach mac Urmi, and it is from Curir Ulad that Ulster derives its name.

There was now the case of the exile of the sons of Uisliu:

The men of Ulster were busy drinking in the house of Conchobor's storyteller, Fedlimid mac Daill. His wife was organizing matters and looking after them, and she was full with child. Food was passed around, and a drunken disturbance shook the place. When the men were ready to sleep the woman retired to her bed. As she crossed the floor, the child cried out in her womb and this cry was heard all over the enclosure. Everyone in the house started up, staring at one another.

The noise was traced, and the woman was brought before the men.

Her husband said, "Woman, what was the noise in your troubled womb. What was the weird uproar at your waist that hurt the ears of all who heard it?"

His heart trembled because he thought the unborn child must have suffered some great terror or some cruel injury.

Fedlimid's wife turned, troubled, to the seer Cathbad.

"Fair-faced Cathbad, hear me, prince, pure, precious crown grown fat with Druid spells . . ." she said.

She could not find adequate words to say what she wanted to say.

Then Cathbad told her that a woman with twisted yellow tresses, and eyes of great beauty had a child hollow in the womb, and Ulster's chariot-warriors would deal many blows for that child. Heroes would fight for her and high kings die on her account. Then, west of Conchobor's kingdom, a great number of fighting men would come. High queens, he said, will envy her lips of Parthian-red opening on her pretty teeth, and her pure, perfect body. Cathbad placed his hand on the woman's stomach, and the baby wriggled.

"Yes," he said, "there is a girl there, and Deirdre shall be her name, but she will bring evil."

When the baby was born, Cathbad said that much damage would follow. In her time, he said, Ulster would be tormented; there would be jealously and the three sons of Uisliu will be exiled. He predicted that in her lifetime a bitter blow would be struck at Emain Macha, and remorse experienced for the ruin wrought by the great son of Róich. He added that Fergus would be exiled because of her and as a result of the much-wept wound of Fiachna, Conchobor's son. Harsh, hideous deeds would be done in anger in the name of the High King and there would be graves everywhere.

Conchobor was advised to kill the child, but he said no. The men of Ulster did not dare to speak out against him.

Deirdre was reared by Conchobor, and she grew up into the loveliest woman in Ireland. She was kept in a secret place, so that no Ulsterman might see her until she was ready to make love to Conchobor. No one was allowed into the enclosure but her foster-father, her foster-mother, and a tall and crooked man called Leborcham, who could not be kept out.

One day in winter, the girl's foster-father was skinning a milk-fed calf on the snow outside their dwelling, and she saw a raven drinking the blood. She said to Leborcham that she might desire a man with hair like a raven, cheeks like blood and a body like snow. She said she would be ill until she saw him.

Noisiu was chanting by himself one day near Emain Macha, on the rampart of the stronghold, and the chanting of the sons of Uisliu sounded sweet to the ear. Every cow or beast that heard it gave two-thirds more milk, and men were filled with peace. Their deeds in war were also great: if the entire province of Ulster had come at them at once, the sons of Uisliu would not be beaten. Their swordsmanship was excellent, and they were as swift as hounds.

When Deirdre heard Noisiu, she slipped out quickly to him. He told her that she had a fine heifer. She replied that heifers grow big where there are no bulls. He said that she had the bull of Ulster all to herself. She said that given the choice she would pick a game young bull like his. He referred to Cathbad's prophecy, and she wanted to know if he was rejecting her.

"I am," he said.

She rushed at him and caught his ears – symbols of shame and mockery.

He cried out, "Woman, leave me alone."

When they heard this, the men of Ulster stared at one another, and Uisliu's other sons went out to their brother. They wanted to know what was wrong, and they said that Ulstermen should not kill one another for bulls. He told them what had happened, and the warriors said that evil would come of it. However, they would not be shamed as long as they lived. There would be no king in Erin that would deny them a welcome.

They left that night with 150 women and the same number of hounds and slaves. Deirdre was amongst them, and she associated with everyone.

They travelled about the island for some time, under protection. Conchobor tried to destroy them with many ambushes and treachery. They travelled round south-eastward from the red cataract at Es Ruaid, and to the promontory at Benn Etair. The men of Ulster pursued them until they crossed the North Channel to Scotland, or Alba. Here they settled in desolate places. When the mountain game ran out, they started raiding cattle. Now the warriors of Alba set out to destroy them. Eventually, they offered themselves to the King of Alba, who accepted them as mercenaries. They built their houses on the green in such a way that no one could look in and see Deirdre as they feared there might be bloodshed on her account.

Early one morning, however, someone entered Noisiu's house without knocking and saw Deirdre sleeping. The man was a steward, and he told the King he had seen a woman with Noisiu mac Uisliu who was fit for a king. The King instructed the steward to try to persuade her to betray Noisiu, but she refused, and she told Noisiu what was afoot. Subsequently the sons of Uisliu were lured into all sorts of traps. Battles took place and the carnage was great, but the brothers always survived. The King tried one last time to seduce Deirdre.

Fearing for their lives, at last the brothers left Scotland and reached an island in the sea. When news of them reached Conchobor, he gave them a guarantee of safety. He decided it would be better to forgive and protect them – to save their lives and let them come home – rather than for enemies to lay them low.

When this news was brought to the brothers, they asked that Fergus should come with them as a pledge of safety, along with Dubthach and Cormac, son of Conchobor.

Before long they were brought back to Ireland, but Fergus became separated from them as a result of Conchobor's cunning. He was invited to many ale feasts, and, owing to an old oath, he could not refuse. The sons of Uisliu had sworn that they would eat nothing in Ireland until they ate Conchobor's food, so they were bound to travel on. Fiachna, Fergus's son, went with them while Fergus and Dubthach stayed behind.

Eventually the sons of Uisliu came to the green at Emain Macha, and Eogan mac Durthacht, King of Fernmag was present. He had come to make peace with Conchobor, who had been his long-term enemy, and he had been chosen to kill Noisiu. Conchobor's soldiers gathered around him so that the sons of Uisliu could not attack him. They stood in the middle of the green, and the women settled on the ramparts of Emain Macha.

Eogan crossed the green with his soldiers, and Fergus's son stood at Noisiu's side. Eogan welcomed Noisiu with a thrust of his spear that broke his back. Fergus's son grasped Noisiu in his arms and threw himself across him. Slaughter and killing broke out all over the green – no one could avoid the conflict.

Deirdre was brought over to Conchobor's side, and she stood beside him with her hands bound behind her back.

Fergus, Dubthach and Cormac came as soon as they heard the news. Dubthach slew Maine, Conchobor's son. Fiachna, son of Conchobor's daughter, Fedelm, was killed with one thrust. Fergus killed Traigthrén, Traiglethan's son, and his brother. Conchobor was outraged. At length 300 men of Ulster fell in battle. Before morning broke Dubthach had killed the girls of Ulster and Fergus had burned Emain Macha.

They went to Connaught, to Ailill and Maeve. This was not a home for Ulstermen, but they knew they would be safe there. They numbered 3,000. For sixteen years in Ulster their weeping and trembling never died away. There was weeping and trembling every night.

During this time Deirdre never smiled, nor ate enough food, nor slept, nor lifted up her hands from her knees. She exclaimed that sweet was the sight of the raiding men returning from Emain Macha. More nobly strode the three proud sons of Uisliu as they rode towards him. Ardan had a stag or boar, and Anle was shouldering a load. The sons of Nes were battle-proud and drank the best mead. Modest Noisiu prepared a cooking-pit on the forest floor. Deirdre said that for him the times were good, and she swore that day that she could not imagine sweeter airs, though Conchobor, their king, may take delight in pipers and trumpeters.

Noisiu's voice was sweet; Ardan was a bright baritone; Anle was a high tenor. Noisiu's grave-mound was made with mourning. She loved his cropped gold fleece. She loved the mighty warrior, loved his firm desire, loved him at daybreak as he dressed by the side of the forest. His blue eyes charmed women and menaced enemies. With their forest journey done, he chanted through the dark woods. He did not sleep much. Perhaps the son of Indel would not come. He did not sleep, but lay there half the night. The crowds drove him out of his mind, and he could neither eat nor smile. He had no use of welcomes now that the nobles were crowding into Emain Macha. There was no comfort, peace or joy, nor mansion nor pleasant ornament.

If Conchobor tried to sooth her, she would chant a poem. She would ask Conchobor what he was thinking about if he was sorrowing. However long he lived he could not spare much love – the thing most dear to him in the world was unreachable. All he saw was fair flesh so bright among the others. His figure stood out amongst Alba's fighting men. He wore a handsome crimson cloak and a multitude of jewels. He carried upon himself for decoration fifty ounces of light gold. He carried a gold-hilted sword as well as two javelins with sharp tips, a shield rimmed with yellow gold with a knob of silver in the middle. Fergus had brought them over the great sea. Now he sold his honour for a drink. Of all Ulster's warriors assembled on the plain Conchobor valued Noisiu most highly. He would gladly have given all the others for Noisiu, son of Uisliu, but in a short while he would be no more. Grief was heavier than the sea.

Conchobor asked Deirdre what she saw that she hated the most.

"You surely," she said, "and Eogan mac Durthacht."

Conchobor said she should go and live for a year with Eogan. Next day they set out for the fair at Emain Macha. She was behind Eogan in the chariot. She had sworn that the two men would never possess her.

"This is good," said Conchobor. "Between me and Eogan you are like a sheep eyeing two rams."

A large black stone was in front of her, and she let her head be driven against the stone until she was dead.

Chapter 2

The Birth of Cúchulainn

Conchobor and his nobles were present at Emain Macha when a flock of birds came and ate all the crops and spoilt the pastureland. The men of Ulster were up in arms as they saw their lands ruined, and they got nine chariots ready to chase away the enemy – they were practised hunters of birds. Conchobor mounted a chariot with his sister Deichtine, and she drove the chariot for her brother. The Ulster warriors, including Conall and Laegaire, arrived in their chariots, along with Bricriu.

Birds flew before them, guiding the way. There were no dykes or fences or stone walls in Ireland at that time, only open plains. The flight of the birds was relaxing and lovely as they sang. There were nine score of them with a silver chain between each couple. Each score went in its own flight – nine flights altogether. Two birds were out in front of each flight with a yoke of silver between them. As night fell three birds separated from the others. The men of Ulster went on until they reached Brug on the Boann river. It snowed heavily, and Conchobor told his men to unyoke their chariots and start looking for shelter.

Conall and Bricriu at length found a solitary house, newly built, where they found a couple and were made welcome. When they returned to their own band, Bricriu said it was useless to go there unless they brought their own food and set the table themselves. However, they went with all their chariots, and were packed into the house. As usual, at meal-time the men of Ulster became drunk.

After a while the man of the house declared that his wife was in her birth pangs in the storeroom. Deichtine attended her and helped her to give birth. At the same time a mare at the door of the house gave birth to two foals. The Ulstermen took charge of the baby boy and gave him the foals as a present. Deichtine nursed him.

As morning broke there was nothing to be seen eastward of Brug – no house or birds, only their own horses, the baby and foals.

They returned to Emain Macha and cared for the baby until he reached boyhood, but he fell ill and died. They performed a lamentation for him, and Deichtine's grief was great. She grew thirsty and asked for a drink, which was brought in a cup. As she drank, a tiny creature slipped into her mouth with the liquid, and she swallowed it.

That night she dreamt that a man came towards her, speaking to her, saying that she would be with child by him, and that the child was to be called Setanta. He told her that he himself was Lug mac Ethnenn, and he said that the foals should be raised with the boy.

The woman became pregnant, and Ulster was alive with speculation about who its father was. Some said Conchobor might be responsible.

Conchobor gave his sister in marriage to one Sualdam mac Róich. She did not like the idea of going to bed, pregnant, with her husband, and she became sick when she reached the bedstead.

The men of Emain Macha were gathered together when her son was born, and they started to argue about who should rear the boy. They approached Conchobor for a decision.

"You should have the boy," Conchobor said to his sister Finnchaem.

Finnchaem looked at the boy and said, "My heart is full of love for him already, as though he were my own Conall Cernach."

Bricriu said that one was his own son and the other his sister's son.

"Take the boy to Conchobor," he said again to his sister, "to be reared."

He said that he was strong and skilful, and that he was noble and nimble in combat. He was also sage, knowing and careful. He had precedence over others when speaking with the King, and he advised him before he spoke. He was the judge of all combats before the battle-proud Conchobor. He settled all cases in Ulster and offended no one. No one but Conchobor could equal him as a foster-father.

One Blai Briuga said that the boy would be safe from harm and neglect. He said he could hold all the men of Ireland in his house and feed them for a week or ten days. In their rashness he could sustain them. In times of insult and trials of honour he would support them. But let his just claim be settled as Conchobor desired.

"Have you no respect?" said Fergus.

He was strong and skilful and a king's messenger. No one could match him for rank or riches. He was a courageous fellow and skilled in arms. His honour was foremost, and he said he was made to look after foster-sons. He sheltered the miserable and watched over the weak.

Amargin said that he was worthy to bring up a king, and that he had many good qualities – he had wisdom and wealth, eloquence and openness of mind, and his family were known for their splendour and courage. If he was not already a prince, he said, he would be worthy as a poet of royal favour. He could kill any chariot-fighter. He looked for no one's thanks but Conchobor's, and he was bound to no one but the King.

Conchobor said that there was nothing to be gained from this. He said that Finnchaem should have the boy until they reached Emain Macha, so that the judge, Morann, could decide.

They set out for Emain Macha, and when they arrived Morann pronounced judgment. He said that the boy should be given to Conchobor, for he was Finnchaem's kin. Senchan could teach him eloquence, Blai Briuga could provide for him, Fergus could take him on his knee, Amargin could be his teacher, with Conall Cernach as his foster-brother. In such a way he would be bound by all his friends – chariot-fighters, princes and sages. This boy would be cherished by many, and would settle trials of honour and win battles.

He was given to Amargin and Finnchaem and reared at Imrith Fort on Murtheimne Plain.

The men of Ulster gathered with Conchobor at Emain Macha, where they drank a lot. The vat could hold 100 measures of coal-black alcohol – enough to satisfy the men of Ulster for the whole evening. The length of the house from one door to another was a total of 105 feet. The warriors performed great feats with their javelins and swords. Their names were Conall Cernach, 'the Triumphant', son of Amargin; Fergus mac Róich, 'the Bravest of the Brave'; Laegaire Buadach, 'the Victorious', son of Connad; Celtchar mac Uthidir; Dubthach mac Lugdach; Cúchulainn mac Sualdam; and Scél, the son of Bairdene, the doorkeeper at Emain Macha.

Cúchulainn heard of his feats of bravery, and the women of Ulster were filled with admiration and love of him. He had a fine face and becoming figure.

Cúchulainn had no wife at this time, and the men of Ulster gathered together to talk about him and about their wives' and daughters' passion for him. They feared that Cúchulainn might die young and leave no heir, which would be tragic. It was only through an heir that Cúchulainn might perpetuate his bloodline. For this reason he should have a woman.

Chapter 3

Cúchulainn's Courtship of Emer

Conchobor sent nine men into the provinces of Ireland looking for a woman for Cúchulainn, and they looked in every fort and town of importance in the country for the daughter of a king, a nobleman or landowner. But after a year the men came back without finding a girl that would suit him.

Cúchulainn went to a place called the Gardens of Lug to court a girl called Emer. She was the daughter of Forgall Monach, known as 'the Cunning'. Cúchulainn and his charioteer set out, and no other chariot could match his for fire and speed. Cúchulainn went up to the girl when she was out on the green with her foster-sisters, the daughters of landowners who lived around Forgall's fort. They were studying embroidery and fine stitching with Emer. Cúchulainn hailed the girls and Emer lifted up her pretty face.

She recognised Cúchulainn and said to him, "May your road be blessed."

He replied, "May the apple of your eye see only good."

For a while they spoke together in riddles. Cúchulainn caught sight of the girl's breasts over the top of her dress. He said that he saw a sweet country where he could rest his weapons.

Emer answered him: "No man may travel to this country until he has killed 100 men at many fords on the River Ailbine."

Cúchulainn said again that in that sweet country he would rest his weapons.

She said that no man would travel there until he had performed the salmon leap carrying twice his weight in gold. Three groups of nine men could be struck down, leaving the middle man of each nine unharmed.

Cúchulainn again said that in that sweet country he would rest his weapons.

She said that no man would travel the country from Samhain when summer came to an end, until Imbolc, when the ewes were milked at the start of spring, or from Imbolc to Beltane to Bron Trogain, the start of the autumn.

Cúchulainn declared that all things had been said and done, and he ended his journey and slept at Emain Macha that night.

The girls told their father how the great Cúchulainn had arrived in his chariot, and about the talk with its hidden meanings that passed between himself and Emer. Forgall said he had seen Cúchulainn going northward across Breg Plain. The landlords told it all to Forgall Monach, with everything that Emer said.

Emer had fallen in love with Cúchulainn, but Cúchulainn said that it would serve no purpose. He decided to put an end to it, because he thought they would never have what they wanted.

Now Forgall travelled to Emain Macha dressed in Gaulish clothes. He said that royal messengers from Gaul wished to speak to Conchobor.

There were three messengers carrying a tribute of gold and Gaulish wine and other presents, and they were given a great welcome. On the third day Forgall sent his people away.

Cúchulainn and Conall Cernach and other Ulster warriors were highly praised in his presence, and he agreed that they fought well – though Cúchulainn now in Scotland would fight more marvellously if he visited Scáthach ('the shadowy one') and studied the warrior arts with her. He could beat any hero in Europe. This he suggested in the event that Cúchulainn would never come back. He believed that if Cúchulainn should marry Emer, somewhere, through the warrior's wildness and ferocity, he himself would meet his death. Cúchulainn said he would approach Forgall. After he had obtained what he wanted, he started out for home.

Next morning Cúchulainn rose up and set out to keep his promise. First he crossed the Breg Plain to see Emer and talk with her before he set sail. She understood that it was Forgall who had been in Emain Macha and that he started to learn warfare, and to keep them apart. She told Cúchulainn he should act with caution, for Forgall would try to destroy him wherever he went. Each of them promised to remain pure until they met again. They bade farewell to each other and looked towards Scotland.

He stayed with Domnall and was taught first the pierced flagstone, with the bellows blowing under it. He danced on it until his soles were blackened. He then climbed up a long spear and performed on its point without causing his soles to bleed. At last Domnall told Cúchulainn that his training would not be finished until he visited Scáthach in the east of Scotland.

So at length Cúchulainn travelled across Scotland to the camp where were present Scáthach's pupils. He asked of her whereabouts and he was told that she might be found on an island. He asked how he could get to her.

"By the Pupil's Bridge," they said, "but no one can cross it unless he is skilled in arms."

The bridge was low at each end and high in the middle. No sooner did he step on it than the other end flew up at him and struck him on his back. Cúchulainn tried to cross the bridge three times, but each time he failed. The men jeered at him, but he performed his hero's salmon leap on to the middle. He reached the far end of the bridge so quickly that it had no time to fly up at him. He sprang on to the solid ground of the island and went up to the fort. He struck the gate with his spear point and broke in.

Scáthach was told about this, and she said that Cúchulainn must have received his training somewhere else. She sent her daughter Uathach to meet the young man, to see who he might be. Uathach saw him and fell silent. Her desire was awakened for him. She gazed at him and returned to her mother. She praised the man whom she had seen. Her mother said she could see that he pleased her, and the girl replied, "Yes, indeed!"

Scáthach said she should take him to bed that night, if that was what she wanted. It would be no problem, she said, if he would like to make love.

The girl looked after him. She gave him water and food, and entertained him, pretending to be a servant.

At last Cúchulainn got hold of her, but while he was overpowering her he hurt her finger, and she cried out. Everyone in the fort heard her and they all started up. One of Scáthach's warriors attacked Cúchulainn and they fought for some time. The warrior tried his special tricks of battle, but Cúchulainn mastered these without effort.

Scáthach mourned when she heard of this, but Cúchulainn said he would assume the duties of the dead man – he would lead her army and be her champion.

Uathach conversed at length with Cúchulainn. After three days the girl told him, if he was serious about learning heroic deeds, he would have to go where Scáthach was teaching her two sons, Cúar and Cat. Cúchulainn placed his sword between her breasts and made her promise three things: thoroughness in training, a dowry for her marriage, and tidings for the future, for Scáthach was also a prophetess.

Cúchulainn went to Scáthach. He stood with his feet on the edges of the weapon chest and the point of his sword against her heart, exclaiming that death was hanging over her. She said that she would give him any three things and Cúchulainn made her promise.

Uathach lived with Cúchulainn, and Scáthach trained him in the arts of war.

While Cúchulainn was training with Scáthach in Scotland and living with her daughter Uathach, another important man in Munster, a foster-brother of Cúchulainn, Lugaid mac Nois, travelled eastwards with twelve chariot-warriors, all princes of

Munster, to make love to the twelve daughters of Coirpre Niafer mac Rus Ruad. However, the girls were already betrothed. Forgall Monach learned of this and travelled to Temair. He said to Lugaid that he had an unmarried daughter who was the prettiest girl in the whole of Ireland. Lugaid was pleased to see her. Forgall promised the girl to him and offered the Breg landowners' twelve daughters to Lugaid's twelve princes.

The King was invited to Forgall's fort for the wedding. Emer was brought to sit beside Lugaid, but she held his cheeks and swore on her life that it was Cúchulainn she loved. She told him she was under Cúchulainn's protection. If anyone else took her it would be a crime against honour.

Lugaid did not dare sleep with Emer for dread of Cúchulainn, and he turned for home.

At this time, Scáthach was in another territory, whose chief was also a woman, Aife. Their two armies faced each other.

Scáthach gave Cúchulainn a sleeping draught and tied him up. This would keep him out of mischief, she thought, but after an hour Cúchulainn sprang up. The draught, which should have lasted him twenty-four hours, had lasted only one.

Cúchulainn started out with Scáthach's two sons against three of Aife's soldiers – Cúar, Cat and Crufe, who were the three sons of Ilsúanach – and he slew them in battle.

The battle started again next morning, and the two forces met face-to-face. Three of Aife's soldiers challenged Scáthach's two sons to combat. They chose the rope of feats. Scáthach sighed, not knowing what would happen to her sons. They were only two men against three. Aife was reputed to be the hardest women in the world.

Cúchulainn joined Scáthach's two sons. He sprang on the cord and killed the three enemy warriors.

Aife challenged Scáthach to single combat. Cúchulainn went to Scáthach and asked her what Aife held most dear. Scáthach said that it was her two horses, and her charioteer.

Cúchulainn fought Aife on the rope of feats, and Aife smashed

Cúchulainn's weapon. All that was left of his sword was no bigger than a fist, but Cúchulainn cried out that Aife's charioteer and her two horses had fallen into the valley and were all dead. Aife looked around and Cúchulainn seized her by her breasts. He took her on his back like a sack and brought her back to his own army. He tossed her to the ground and held a sword over her.

Cúchulainn said, "A life for a life. Grant me three desires," he said. Aife told him that what he wanted in one breath he would obtain. His desires were hostages for Scáthach, Aife's promise never to attack her again, her company that night at her own fort, and for her to bear him a son. She said that she would grant all his requests.

Cúchulainn slept the night with Aife, and soon she was pregnant. She said that if she gave birth to a boy, in seven years' time she would send him to Ireland.

Cúchulainn left the boy a gold thumb ring and told her that the boy should come to Ireland to find him when his finger grew too big for the ring. He gave him the name of Connla, and said that Connla was to reveal this name to no one, and that he should refuse no man in combat.

On his way back to Ireland, Cúchulainn met a one-eyed hag on a cliff path. She told him to get out of the way, but there was no room to pass. In the end he let her have the path, except where he clung with his toes. She struck at his big toe as she passed him by, so that he would be knocked off the cliff. However, he saw her just in time and performed his hero's salmon leap upward. Then he struck at the hag's head. She was Eis Enchenn, the bird-headed mother of the last three warriors to die at his hands. She wanted to avenge their deaths, so she had lain in wait for him.

Scáthach and her men returned to their own land with the hostages that Aife had given them. Cúchulainn waited there until his wounds had healed.

When Cúchulainn's training in the arts of war with Scáthach was completed, he was able to juggle nine apples with never more than one on his palm; he could perform the thunder-feat, the feats of the sword-edge and the sloped shield, the feats of the javelin and rope, the body feat, the feat of cat and the heroic salmon-leap, the pole-throw and the leap over a poisoned stake, the breath feat (with golden apples thrown up into the air), the hero's scream, the stroke of precision and the cry-stroke. He could step on a lance in flight. He could ride the sickle-chariot and truss a warrior on the point of a spear.

Word came to him to return to his own country, so he bade them goodbye. Scáthach spoke to him of his future, and also his end. She chanted to him through the Light of Foresight. She told him that she saluted him, weary in triumph and battle-eager.

"Go where you will find some comfort," she said, and she made many predictions.

No matter where he stood danger was ever at hand. She would be alone and troubled by envy. Cruachan's heroes he would destroy. Some heroes would lie defeated. His straight sword would hang behind him stained with Setanta's gore. Battle would rage and bones would be broken with the spear. Cattle would be stolen out of Breg and his country would be under bondage, with cattle straying on the ways for five long days. His blood would be a red plague splashed on many shields. The crows would scour the ploughed ground and the savage kites would be found. Herds would be broken up in wrath, and great armies would drive the hordes. Blood would be spilt in a great flood, and Cúchulainn's body would become wasted. There would be bitter wounds to bear.

With his red stabbing spear he would experience grief and sorrow – murderous moments on the plain, playing at the stabbing game. Now the champion came in rage, heroic in his great acts, along with harsh screams and a cruel heart. Let him come and kill women and let Maeve fight with Ailill.

The white horned bull roared against the brown bull of Cúailnge. When would he come? He would complain of weakness. He would arise once more and seize his arms, seasoned in the crafts of war. For Ulster's land and virgin women he would arise now in all his force with warlike and cruel wielding of a strong spear, and also a straight sword dyed red in dark blood. Men in Scotland would know his name, and in the winter night he would take pity on them.

Cúchulainn returned to Emain Macha and related all his adventures. After he was rested he headed towards Forgall's ramparts in Luglochta Logo to find Emer. There was a strong guard about her, and for a whole year he had not been able to contact her. Now he faced Forgall's forces in earnest. The sickle-chariot was harnessed for him, and he drove it into battle. That day he killed 309 men.

He reached Forgall's ramparts and performed his salmon leap across the three enclosures in the centre of the fort. At the inner enclosure he dealt three strokes at three groups of nine men. He slew eight men at each stroke and left one man standing in the middle of each group. These were Emer's three brothers, Scibar, Ibor and Cat. Forgall retreated in flight from Cúchulainn, out across the forts, but he fell and killed himself.

Cúchulainn caught Emer and her foster-sister with their weight in gold and silver, and leaped again with the girls across the rampart. He hurried away with shrieks rising around them on all sides. Scenmenn's Ford was the place where Scenmenn died.

Cúchulainn and the two women came to Glondáth, where Cúchulainn slew 100 men. Cúchulainn said that Glondáth ('ford of the deed'), would be its name for ever.

At length Cúchulainn reached Crúfóit, which means 'the white plain'. He delivered great blows to the assembled army there, and blood poured out on every side.

"You have made a hill of bloody sods today, Cúchulainn," Emer said.

After this it was called Sod of the Blood.

The pursuers came up with them on the Boann river. Emer got out of her chariot and Cúchulainn gave chase northwards over the ford. The sods flew from the horses' hoofs. Cúchulainn killed 100 men at every ford between Ath Scenmenn and Ailbine to the Baonn river at Berg, doing all that he had promised the girl. He reached Emain Macha by nightfall.

Emer was brought before Cúchulainn and the other Ulster chieftains, and they made her welcome. There was present Bricriu mac Carbad, a sharp-tongued fellow, who said that Cúchulainn would find the night's doings very hard: the woman he had brought would have to sleep with Conchobor.

Cúchulainn became wild at this. He trembled so much that his cushion burst under him, and the feathers blew around the house. He rushed out.

"This could be very troublesome," Cathbad said. "Cúchulainn will kill any man who sleeps with his wife."

Conchobor said to call Cúchulainn back, and he would try to calm him down.

Cúchulainn returned and Conchobor said he should bring back the herds about Sliab Fuait.

Cúchulainn went and gathered together all the animals he could find at Sliab Fuait. He drove them in one flock to the green at Emain Macha, and his anger had gone.

The men of Ulster discussed the matter and decided that Emer should sleep in Conchobor's bed, but with Fergus and Cathbad in it as well in order to protect Cúchulainn's honour. They declared that all Ulster would bless the couple if Cúchulainn accepted this arrangement. He did so, and Conchobor paid Emer's dowry the next day. Cúchulainn was given his 'honour prize', and he slept ever after with his wife. They did not part again until they died.

Chapter 4

Aife's Son Dies

Why did Cúchulainn kill his own son?

Seven years to the day after Cúchulainn had left Aife, the boy came looking for his father. The men of Ulster were assembled at Tracht Esi, and they saw the boy rowing towards them, looking for his father. He had travelled over the sea in a small boat of bronze, and he had the gilt oars in his hands. There was a pile of stones beside him in the boat. He placed a stone in his sling and sent it humming through the air. The stone stunned a bird without killing it, and he let it escape into the air again. Then he used his voice to bring the birds down a second time.

Conchobor said he pitied the boy because of the country he was heading to. The boy did not know the land he came from, and he feared that the Ulstermen would grind him into dust.

"Someone should go out to meet him, and not let him ashore," he said. "Condere mac Echach should go."

"Why Condere?" they all asked.

Conchobor said that this was a situation requiring good sense and eloquence, and Condere was the right person.

Condere went up to the boy just as he reached the strand.

"Young man," said Condere, "where have you come from and who are your folk?"

The boy said he would give his name to no one, but Condere

34

said he could not allow him to land unless he gave his name. The boy said he was going where he was going. The boy moved to pass Condere, but Condere said that mighty deeds were his, and he had the pride of an Ulster warrior. Conchobor would protect him. But the boy threatened Condere and the others with a little spear.

"Let Conchobor grant you protection," said Condere. "Listen and pay attention. Come to Conchobor, and to Sencha mac Ailella, who was boasting of his victories."

"He must go to Fintan's son, Cethern of the Crimson Blade, the fire that burns battalions. He must go to the poet Amargin and to Cúscraid of the great armies. He must come with care of Conall Cernach above story and song," the heroes shouted together.

"Insults would hurt him. Come – let it be said," Condere urged.

He arose and approached the warlike boy.

Condere said that he would oppose him, a beardless, unfledged boy, if he did not heed the men of Ulster.

"You have come and spoken well," the boy said.

Then he used his voice and his spear with such skill that he gathered a lovely flock of birds.

"I have sworn that no man will stand in my way," he told the Ulsterman. "I am prepared to fight you, singly or together. Turn aside, for even if you have the strength of 100 men, you will not hold me back."

Condere returned to the men of Ulster and told them what had happened. He said that no one would make little of Ulster as long as he lived. He said that he would not permit it.

Conall went out to meet the lad.

"Those were pretty games," Conall told the boy.

The boy said they would work as well for him as for the birds. He placed a stone in his sling and sent it into the sky. The stone knocked Conall headlong, and before he could rise the boy had his shield-strap tied around Conall's arms.

"Send out someone else!" Conall exclaimed.

The entire army was put to shame, until at last Cúchulainn approached the boy, performing feats as he went. Emer had her arm round his neck, and she said that he should not murder his son. He should remember Scáthach's strict warning and turn from this folly. Cúchulainn knew that the boy was Connla, his and Aife's only son.

Cúchulainn continued: "Be quiet, wife. No matter who he is, I must kill him for the honour of Ulster."

He went down to meet the boy.

"Those were pretty games," he said.

The young boy answered that they were pretty games that he found here.

"Maybe you were meant to meet me?" said Cúchulainn. "Name yourself or you will die."

"So be it," the boy answered.

The boy attacked Cúchulainn and they struck at each other. The boy cut him bald-headed with one stroke of his sword.

Cúchulainn said it was now time for them to wrestle, but the boy said he could not reach up to Cúchulainn's belt. He climbed on to two standing stones, and, without moving a foot, he thrust Cúchulainn three times between the two stones. His feet sank in the stones up to his ankles, and the marks of his feet are there to this day, which is why the people of Ulster call it the Strand of the Mark.

They went down to the sea to drown each other, and the boy submerged Cúchulainn twice. Now Cúchulainn turned and played foul in the water with the feats that Scáthach had taught him. He sent a weapon speeding over the water at the boy and brought his bowels down around his feet.

The boy said that Cúchulainn had wounded him woefully, and Cúchulainn agreed that he had. He took the boy in his arms and carried him before the people of Ulster. He laid the boy down and saluted the men of Ulster.

"Here you are – the boy," he said.

"Alas! Alas!" cried all of Ulster.

"It is the truth," the boy said. "If I only had five years amongst you I would slaughter the warriors of all the world: I would look as far away as Rome."

He asked Cúchulainn to point out the famous men around him, for he wanted to salute them. He placed his arms round the neck of each man in turn, and hailed his father, but then he died. A loud lament was uttered up for him. His grave was made and the gravestone set. For three days and three nights no calf in Ulster was let go to his cow on account of Connla's death.

Chapter 5

Quarrels and Bulls

There was a dispute between Ochall of Connaught and Bodb, King of Munster. They had two pig-keepers called Friuch, after a boar's bristle, and Rucht, after its grunt. Friuch was Bodb's pig-keeper and Rucht was Ochall's pig-keeper. They were both trained in pagan arts and could form themselves into any shape, like Morgan mac Fiachna. When the acorns and beechmast fell in Munster, Rucht would take his pigs down there. When the mast fell in Connaught, Friuch would travel northward.

Some tried to make trouble between them. The people of Connaught said that Rucht had the greater power, whilst in Munster they said Friuch had the greater power.

One year when Rucht travelled southwards with his pigs. Men said that Friuch would cast a spell over Rucht's pigs, so that, even though they ate, they would not grow fat, while Friuch's own pigs would flourish. This is what happened. In the end, Rucht was forced to take his pigs away with him, and they were so wretched that they could barely make it home. Everyone laughed at him when he returned. They said it was a bad day when he had set out, and Friuch must have greater power than he had.

"It proves nothing," Rucht answered.

Some time later, Friuch came into the province of Connaught, bringing his lean pigs with him. The same thing happened in reverse, and Friuch came back from the north with his pigs in poor condition. Bodb dismissed him from pig-keeping, and Rucht was dismissed by Ochall.

After this they had to spend two years in the shape of birds of prey. They spent the first year at Cruachan, in North Connaught, and the second on Femen Plain in Munster.

One day the men of Munster were gathered together at this place. They said the birds were making a terrible noise there. They had been behaving like that for a year. As they were talking they saw Fuidell mac Fiadmire, Ochall's steward, approaching them up the hill, and they made him welcome. They remarked upon the noise of the birds, and Fuidell said they could be the same two birds they had seen in the north the year before.

After spending two full years in the shape of birds, during which time they spent a year at Cruachan and a year at Femen Plain, so that all men had seen their power, they had to take the shape of water creatures and live for two years in the Sinann and Siuir rivers.

They then turned into two stags, and each led a herd of deer. Then they took the form of warriors and fought with each other; then two phantoms, terrifying each other; then two dragons, pouring down snow on each other's land. Eventually they dropped down out of the air, and became two maggots. One of them got into the spring of the River Cronn in Cúailnge, where a cow belonging to Dáire mac Fiachna drank. They managed to get into the wellspring at Garad in Connaught. Here a cow belonging to Maeve and Ailill drank them up. The result was the two bulls – Finnbennach, the white horned bull of Ai Plain, and Donn Cúailnge, the brown bull of Cúailnge.

Rucht and Friuch were their names when they were pig-keepers; Ingen and Ette ('talon' and 'wing') when they were birds of prey; Bled and Bolod ('whale' and 'sea beast') when they were two water creatures; Rinn and Faebur ('point' and 'edge') when they were warriors; Scáth and Sciath ('shadow' and 'shield') when they were phantoms; and Cruinniuc and Tuinniuc when they were maggots.

The brown bull of Cúailnge was haughty, healthy, horrific, ferocious and full of craft. It was brave and thick-breasted with curly hair and it held its head high. Its neck was thick and strong. It had a typical bull's brow and a wave's sound and a royal wrath and the rush of a bear. It had a beast's rage and a bandit's stab, with a lion's fury. Thirty grown boys could take their place from rump to nape. He was a foolhardy hero. He was the father of great beasts and overlooked the ox of the earth.

Finnbennach had a white head and white feet and a body the colour of blood. It looked as if it had bathed in blood or dyed in the red bog or pounded in purple with his blank paps. He had a heavy mane and great hoofs. He had a ponderous tail and a stallion's breast and a cow's eye and a salmon's snout. He was bound to have victory, bellowing in greatness, the idol of the ox herd, and the prime demon of Ai.

Chapter 6

Pillow Talk

Once upon a time, when the royal bed was made up for Ailill and Maeve at Cruachan in Connaught, they had a talk upon the pillows.

"Is it true?" said Ailill. "Was it well for the wife of a wealthy man?"

"True enough!" she answered. "What put that in your mind?"

"It strikes me", Ailill said, "how much better off you are today than the day that I married you."

Maeve replied that she was well enough without him.

Ailill said that her wealth was something he did not know about; he only knew about her woman's ways. The neighbouring enemies were making off with loot and plunder.

"Not at all!" Maeve said.

The High King of Ireland was Maeve's father, Eochaid Feidlech ('the Steadfast'), who had a long lineage. He outstripped other men in grace and warlike combat. He had 1,500 soldiers in his pay – all exile's sons – and the same number of freeborn native men. For every paid soldier he had ten more men.

Her father gave her a whole province of Ireland, and she ruled it from Cruachan, which was why she was called Maeve of Cruachan. They came from Finn, King of Leinster, Rus Ruad's son, to woo her. They came from Conchobor, King of Ulster, son of Fachtna. They also came from Eochaid Bec. She requested the largest wedding ever held in Ireland. There was an absence of meanness, jealousy and fear. If she married a mean man, the union would be wrong: she herself was full of grace and giving, and it would be an insult if she were more generous than her husband. If her husband was a timid man, the union would be just as wrong because she thrived on all kinds of trouble. It was an insult for a wife to be more spirited than her husband, but it was acceptable for them to be equally spirited. Whenever she was with one man, another was waiting in the shadows.

In the end she got the kind of man she desired: Rus Ruad's other son, Ailill, from Leinster. Maeve was not sluggish, greedy or jealous. When promises were made to her she brought the best wedding gift a bride could bring. There was clothing enough for a dozen men, a chariot worth three times seven bondmaids. There was the width of her face in gold, and the weight of her right arm in light gold. If anyone was to cause shame or upset, the right of compensation was hers, Maeve said, for he was a kept man.

"By no means!" said Ailill, for two of his brothers were kings – Coirpre in Temair and Finn over Leinster. They ruled because of their age; not because they were better than Ailill in grace or giving. He had never heard of a woman running a province in the whole of Ireland, which was why he came and took the kingship. Ailill was the son of Mata Muresc, Mágach's daughter. Who better for his queen than Maeve, a daughter of the High King of Ireland!

Maeve said that her fortune was greater than his.

"You amaze me!" said Ailill, for no one had more property than he had.

Their possessions were brought out, to see who had more assets. There were buckets, tubs, iron pots, jugs, pails and other vessels with handles. There was gold and expensive clothes, and many other valuables. Their herds of sheep were brought in from the fields. In this way their fortunes were measured and matched, and they were found to be the same. For instance, the great lamb leading Maeve's sheep was worth as much as one bondmaid, but there was a ram to match him leading Ailill's sheep.

From pasture and paddock their teams and herds of horses were brought in. For the finest horse in Maeve's stud, Ailill had a stallion to match. The great herds of pigs were brought in from the gullies and waste places, and they also matched. Maeve had one fine boar; Ailill also had one. Their droves and free-wandering herds of cattle were brought in from the forests and wastes of Ulster. These also matched.

However, there was a great bull in Ailill's herd, and it had been a calf of one of Maeve's cows. Finnbennach was its name – the white horned bull. It refused to be led by a woman and had gone over to the King's herd. Maeve could not find in her herd the equal of this bull, and her spirits dropped.

Maeve called for her messenger, Mac Roth, and she asked him to find the match of the bull.

Mac Roth exclaimed that he knew where to find such a bull in Ulster – in the territory of Cúailnge, in Dáire mac Fiachna's house. Donn Cúailnge was the bull's name – the brown bull of Cúailnge.

"Go there," Maeve said, "and ask Dáire for a loan of the bull for a year. At the end of the year he can have fifty yearling heifers as well as the return of the brown bull."

If the people of the country thought badly of losing their fine bull, Maeve would rejoice in a cattle raid. If Dáire himself came with the bull, she agreed to give him part of the fine plain of Ai and a chariot worth three times seven bondmaids.

Messengers were sent out to Dáire's house – and there were nine of them including Mac Roth.

Mac Roth was made welcome in Dáire's house, as befitted Ireland's chief messenger, and he said he had come to ask for the loan of Donn Cúailnge. Mac Roth explained why Maeve wanted the bull and told Dáire he would get fifty yearling heifers in payment for the loan. If he would come with the bull himself, Dáire was offered a portion of the plain of Ai and a chariot worth three times seven bondmaids.

Dáire was so pleased that he jumped for joy until the seams of his cushion burst under him. He cried out that he did not care what the Ulstermen would think – he agreed to take Donn Cúailnge to Ailill and Maeve in Connaught.

Mac Roth and the other messengers were looked after. Fine straw was settled under them, and they were served the best food and drink. Unfortunately they became drunk and boastful. One of the messengers said that if Dáire hadn't agreed to loan them the bull, they would have taken it away anyway.

The man in charge of Dáire mac Fiachna's household overheard what was said, and he reported it straight back to Dáire.

Dáire was furious.

He exclaimed, "By the gods, nothing shall leave here unless I ordain it."

The next morning the messengers went to Dáire's house and asked where they could find Donn Cúailnge.

Dáire said they would not have it, and that it was not his practice to murder messengers but not one of them deserved to leave there alive. He said he would not give up his bull because he knew what the messengers had been saying.

When the messengers returned empty-handed, Mac Roth related what had happened.

Before long, word got around that as the bull had not been given up voluntarily, Maeve intended to take it by force.

Chapter 7

The Army Sets Out

Ailill and Maeve assembled a huge army in Connaught, and they sent word to the other three provinces. Ailill also sent messengers to his brothers, and to the rest of Mágach's seven sons. As well as Ailill there was Anluan, Mugcorb, Cet, En, Bascall and Dóchae, each of them having a troop of 3,000 warriors. Ailill sent word to Conchobor's son, Cormac Connlongas, the leader of the Ulster exiles. His troop of 3,000 were living in Connaught. Soon they arrived at Cruachan Ai.

Cormac marched on Cruachan. He had three companies. The first company wore speckled cloaks and their hair was clipped. Tunics covered them to the knees. They boasted full-length shields and each warrior had a broad grey stabbing spear on a slender shaft. The second company wore dark-grey cloaks and red tunics that reached to their calves. Their hair was swept back upon their heads and they carried bright shields and five-pronged spears. The third troop wore purple cloaks, and red tunics reaching down to their feet. Their hair was trimmed to the shoulder. They carried curved scallop-edged shields and spears.

Men from four of the provinces of Ireland gathered together at Cruachan Ai. Their sages and Druids delayed them for a fortnight, waiting for a sign.

When they finally set out, Maeve said to her charioteer that everyone leaving a lover or a friend would curse her.

"Wait a minute," the charioteer said, and he turned the chariot round to the right and gave the sign for a safe return.

Shortly after this a young grown girl appeared in front of them. She had yellow hair, and she sported a speckled cloak fastened with a gold pin. She also wore a red-embroidered hood and sandals with gold clasps. Her brow was broad and she had dark eyelashes that cast a shadow down her cheeks. Her teeth were in good condition, and she had an impressive shock of hair. She had a light-gold weaving rod in her hand, and her eyes had triple irises. Her chariot was drawn by two black horses, and she was armed.

Maeve asked the girl who she was, and she replied that she was a poet. She also asked the girl where she had come from, and she replied that she had come from Scotland. Maeve asked her if she had the power of foresight, and the girl replied that she had.

Maeve then asked her to predict the fate of her army, and the girl said she saw crimson – perhaps blood. Maeve said this could not be true, for Conchobor was suffering his pangs at Emain Macha along with the other warriors of Ulster. Her messenger had come from Emain Macha and told her. Then Maeve said that wrath and rage and wounds are common when forces gather for battle.

The girl again said she saw red. She said she saw a battle with a blond man with much blood about his belt and a halo around his head. He boasted of many victories. Seven jewels were set in one of his eyes. His jaws were set in a snarl, and he wore a red tunic. He had a noble countenance and his great bravery brought to mind the famous Cúchulainn. The prediction went into terrible detail: entire armies coloured crimson by his hand; a giant on the plain, engaged in battle, holding swords in each of his two hands, or hurling a spear; he towered on the battlefield in his breastplate and red cloak; across his chariot wheel death would be dealt; he would pursue whole armies, dealing destruction and causing great bloodshed – in thousands they would yield their heads. . . .

The Monday after Samhain they set out. They travelled south-east from Cruachan Ai through many regions to Finnabair in Cúailnge. It was at Finnabair that the armies of Ireland later split up across Ulster in order to look for the bull.

Chapter 8

Cúchulainn Sees the Army

On the first stage of their journey they travelled from Cruachan
to Cúil Silinne, at Carrcin Lake. Maeve told her charioteer to
yoke up her nine chariots so that they could make a circuit of the
camp to see who was reluctant to march. Meanwhile Ailill's tent
was pitched and the beds made up. Next to Ailill was Fergus
mac Róich's tent; next to Fergus was Cormac Connlongas,
Conchobor's son; next to him was Conall Cernach; and next to
him was Fiacha mac Fir-Febe, the son of Conchobor's daughter.
A little further on was Finnabair and, next to her, Flidais. Maeve's
tent was on the other side of Ailill.

Maeve came back from inspecting the forces and said that it
would be unwise to proceed with the 3,000 warriors from North
Leinster.

"What fault have you found with them?" asked Ailill.

Maeve said she could find no fault with them, and that they
were fine warriors. By this time they had finished their meal and
the harps were playing.

"It would be foolish to take them," said Maeve. "They will get
all the credit for our efforts."

"But they will be fighting on our side," Ailill replied. "Let them
stay."

Maeve said she had made up her mind – she would get rid of

them and seize their belongings when they were gone.

Ailill asked what they would do with them. Then Maeve said bluntly that she meant to kill them.

Ailill said, "This is a woman's way of thinking – a wicked thing."

Fergus said, "These men are our friends; this is evil advice."

Maeve said she had plenty of men who might do the deed and she pointed out that her army was large enough without the Leinster men. She had her own following of 6,000 men. There were also Maeve's sons, the seven Maines, with their seven troops of 3,000. The seven Maines were Maine Máthramail ('the mother-like'); Maine Athramail ('the father-like'); Maine Morgor ('the strongly dutiful'); Maine Mingor; Maine Milscothach ('of the honeyed speech'); Maine Andoe ('the swift'); and Maine Cotagaib Uli, who was like his mother and father, with the dignity of both. They also had seven Munster kings on their side, each with a troop of 3,000. Altogether in the camp there were seventeen troops of 3,000 each, as well as the general rabble, the young and the women. The eighteenth troop – the Gáleoin – were in the vicinity, and later they were scattered among the army so they would not break up the existing order.

Next morning the army set out for Móin Coltna, a moor near Colatin. Here they stumbled across eight score of wild deer. When they came to Trego Plain, they broke their march and prepared their food.

It is said that Dubthach chanted there: "Take note and listen well to his vision of the war, for a dark march lay ahead towards Ailill's wife's white horn. One man of great note came to guard Murtheimne's herds. Two pig-keepers were friends once, but now crows would drink a cruel milk. The River Cronn would rise and bar the way to Murtheimne until the warrior's work would be done at a mountain in the north. Ailill said to Cormac, "Quick – hurry to your son's side. The cattle were calm on the plains."

Now in due course there was a battle with Maeve and one-third of the army.

The war-spirited Nemain attacked them. They had no peace

that night, and they were kept awake by Dubthach's cries. Groups of men started up and many of the army remained troubled until Maeve came and calmed them down. They spent the night at Gránard in North Tethba.

Fergus sent a warning from there to the men of Ulster – the result of old friendship. They were still suffering from their pangs, but all but Cúchulainn and his father travelled out as far as Iraird Cuillenn. Here they kept watch for the armies. Cúchulainn said he felt the presence of the armies that night, and he must go and warn Ulster. He said that he had promised to spend the night with Fedelm Noichride. Some say, however, that the meeting was with her bondmaid, who was set aside for Cúchulainn's use. Before he left he issued a challenge and cut an ogham message into a stone.

Fergus was appointed the head of the army. He made a substantial detour southward to give Ulster time to assemble an army, and he did this out of old friendship.

Maeve said to Fergus, "There is something wrong. Why do we keep straying into the south or north, crossing every kind of land?"

She suspected that Fergus lacked commitment and she said that perhaps another leader should be chosen.

Fergus answered, "Maeve, what is troubling you? No treachery was meant."

Fergus said he knew every winding way he took.

At length they came to Iraird Cuillenn. Err and Innel with their two charioteers were out in front of the army, keeping their rugs and brooches from being soiled by the dust of the host. They found the spancel-hoop thrown there by Cúchulainn. Sualdam's two horses had bitten the grass, roots and all, out of the earth, while Cúchulainn's horses had licked up the clay, down to the stones beneath the grass. They waited for the armies to come while their musicians played for them.

They gave the spancel-hoop to Fergus mac Róich, and he read the ogham cut into the stone.

When Maeve arrived, she said, "Why are you waiting here?"

Fergus replied that they were waiting because of the spancel-hoop and the ogham message. The message said, 'Come no further, unless you have a man who can make a hoop like this with one hand.' Cúchulainn had excluded his friend Fergus from the challenge.

Fergus called for the Druids and asked them what the riddle of the hoop meant, how many men had put it there, and if it would bring the armies to disaster if they passed on their way.

One of the Druids replied that a great champion had made it and left it as a trap for the warriors – an angry barrier against kings. He said that the host should go no further, unless there was a man amongst them who could make a hoop in the same way.

"If you ignore this challenge and pass by, the rage of the man that cut the ogham will reach you, even if you are under guard or locked in your home."

Ailill said that they should go through the neck of the great forest to the south, so the armies began to cut down the trees to make way for the warriors on their chariots. The place is now called Slechta ('the hewn place').

It is recorded in other books that after they had reached Fid Dúin, the forest fortress, they saw a chariot with a beautiful young girl driving it. This was the prophetess Fedelm, and the forest was cut down after she told Maeve she could not see them properly for the woods.

"It should be made ploughed land," said Maeve. "We will cut down the forest."

The place was named Slechta, and it was here that the Partraigi dwelled.

They spent the night in Cúil Sibrille – Cenannos, as it is now called. Snow fell over the men's belts and chariot wheels. They could not prepare any food and they rose early the following day after spending a troublesome night in the snow.

Cúchulainn had been with his woman, but he rose early and set out to discover the track of the army. When he saw them, he said he wished they had not arrived there and betrayed Ulster.

Cúchulainn went around the forces until he reached Ath Gabla. Here he cut out a tree fork with one stroke of his blade and stuck it in the middle of the stream so that a chariot would have no way of passing. It was from this that the name Ath Gabla comes ('the ford of the forked branch'). Err and Innel, with their two charioteers, came upon him, and he cut off their four heads and tossed them on to the four points of the tree fork.

The horses of the four warriors went back towards the army with their crimson coverings. Everyone thought there was an army waiting for them at the ford, and a troop went forth to inspect the ford. All they found was a single chariot with words in ogham cut into its side. At this, the whole army arrived.

"Do these heads belong to our people?" asked Maeve.

"Yes, they do," Ailill said.

One of the men read out the ogham on the side of the fork. It told them that a single man had thrust the fork into the ground using one hand. They must not go past until one of them – not Fergus – had done the same single-handedly.

Ailill was surprised how easily the four men had been killed.

"That is not what should surprise you," Fergus said. "The fork has been forced into the ground by a single stroke. No hole had been dug to receive it; it has been thrown into the ground from the back of a chariot."

Fergus commanded that the obstruction should be removed, but fourteen chariots broke up trying to drag it out. At last Fergus brought the fork on to dry land with his own chariot and they could see that it had been hewn with a single cut.

Ailill asked Fergus if he thought Conchobor had done this.

Fergus replied, "He has not. He never comes to the border country without a full contingent."

Ailill asked if it could have been Celtchar mac Uthidir.

Fergus replied, "He never comes to the border country without a full battle force."

Ailill asked if it might have been Eogan mac Durthacht.

Fergus replied, "It was not. He would never cross the border without a troop of 3,000 chariots around him. The man who has done this is Cúchulainn. It was he who drove the branch into the ground with a single stroke and killed the four men."

"What sort of man", Ailill asked, "is this Hound of Ulster? How old is this remarkable person?"

Fergus said, "In his fifth year he went in quest of arms to the boy-troop at Emain Macha. In his seventh year he went to study the art of warfare with Scáthach, and he courted Emer. At present he is in his seventeenth year."

Maeve asked, "Is he the most valorous warrior in Ulster?"

Fergus said, "He is the hardest of all. No raven is more flesh-ravenous, no hand more deft, no one of his age is nearly as good, no lion more ferocious, no warrior in battle is more formidable, no hammer is harder. You will find no one to match him."

"Let us not make too much of it," said Maeve, "for he has only one body. He can suffer wounding, and he can't be beyond being captured. He is only in his early youth, and his warrior deeds are yet to come."

Fergus said that although he was a youth his deeds were already manly.

Chapter 9

Cúchulainn's Youthful Deeds

Cúchulainn was reared by his father and mother in their oaken house on Murtheimne Plain. Here he heard great rumours of the boys of Emain Macha. There were three time fifty boys always playing at Emain Macha. Conchobor spent one-third of his royal days watching the boys, one-third playing *fidchell* and one-third drinking ale until he fell asleep. There was no greater warrior in Erin, said Fergus, and he said this even though Cúchulainn had driven him into exile.

Cúchulainn begged his mother to let him join the boy-troop, but his mother said he could not go until there were some Ulster warriors available to go with him. Cúchulainn said this was too long to wait, and he asked to be pointed in the direction of Emain Macha. His mother pointed him to the north and told him it would be a hard road. Sliab Fuait blocked the way. But Cúchulainn said he would try.

He set off with a toy shield made out of sticks, a toy javelin, his hurling stick and a ball. He kept tossing his javelin and catching it again before it hits the ground.

When he arrived at Emain Macha, he ran up to Conchobor's boys without getting them to pledge his safety. They shouted at him, but still he came against them. They flung 150 javelins at him, and he stopped them all with his shield. They drove all their hurling balls at him, and he stopped every ball on his chest. Then they threw their hurling sticks at him – 150 of them – but he dodged them so well that none of them harmed him.

The war-spasm overtook him, and it seemed that each hair was hammered into his head so sharply did they stand upright. He peeled back his lips until his gullet showed. He attacked the boys and killed fifty of them before they could get to the gate of Emain Macha.

Fergus said that he and Conchobor were playing *fidchell*, and Cúchulainn chased nine of the boys across the *fidchell* board. Conchobor caught him by the wrist and asked him what was going on. Cúchulainn said he had left his home, and his mother and father, to join in the games, but the boys had treated him roughly.

"Whose son are you?" Conchobor asked.

He said he was Setanta, son of Sualdam and Conchobor's sister Deichtine.

Conchobor asked why he did not put himself under the boys' protection.

Cúchulainn said he knew nothing of this custom, and he said he was going to offer them his protection.

"Promise it here and now," said Conchobor, and Cúchulainn said he would do so.

Then everyone went out on to the playing fields, and the boys that had been struck down began to get up with the help of their foster-mothers and -fathers.

Fergus said that when Cúchulainn was a boy he could not fall asleep at all in Emain Macha unless his bed was exactly right. Conchobor had a block of stone wrought for his head and another for his feet and provided a special bed for him. One morning a man went to wake him, and Cúchulainn struck him on the forehead with his fist. In doing so, he knocked one of the stone blocks flat with his arm. He had a warrior's fist and the arm of a prodigy. After that time Fergus dared not waken him, but left him to wake up himself.

When they played ball at Emain Macha, Cúchulainn stood alone against 350 boys, and he always beat them. One day one of them managed to lay hold of him, but he worked his fist on him and then knocked fifty of the others down. He took flight and hid under Conchobor's bed. Fergus and thirty other warriors overturned the bed and Cúchulainn was surrounded by the Ulstermen. In the end Fergus settled matters and made peace between the boy-troop and Cúchulainn.

At one time Durthacht challenged the men of Ulster to battle, and the men of Ulster took up the challenge. Cúchulainn was left to sleep, and Ulster was beaten. Conchobor and one of his sons were left for dead and others were heaped about them. Their cries woke Cúchulainn, and he arose and went to the gate of the enclosure, where he met Fergus returning wounded.

"Alas!" he said, "God help you. Where is Conchobor?"

Fergus replied that he did not know.

The night was dark as Cúchulainn made for the field of slaughter. A half-headed man with half a corpse on his back cried out to Cúchulainn to help him to carry his brother's body.

Cúchulainn said he would not, and they began to wrangle, but then they heard someone calling from amongst the corpses. It was a poor warrior lying at the feet of a ghost. Cúchulainn knocked off the half-head with his hurling stick and played ball with it across the battle plain. As he went, he searched for Conchobor.

At last Cúchulainn heard a cry and found Conchobor in a trench. Conchobor asked why he had come to the field of slaughter, and Cúchulainn said that he wished to learn what mortal terror was. He pulled Conchobor out of the trench, though it might have taken six other strong Ulstermen to do the same.

Conchobor asked Cúchulainn to go with him to a nearby house and light a fire for him. When this was done, Conchobor said that if he was given a cooked pig, he might come back to life. Cúchulainn said that he would go and get one.

He came upon a young man by a cooking-pit in the middle of the forest. The man held his weapon in one hand and was cooking a boar with the other. He was a man of great violence, but Cúchulainn attacked him, cut off his head and carried the boar back to Conchobor. Conchobor ate the boar and said it was time to go the rest of the way home.

They found Cúscraid, Conchobor's son, on the way. He lay on the ground in great pain from his wounds. Cúchulainn lifted him on his back and all three headed for Emain Macha.

Another time the men of Ulster were in their pangs. This affliction never affected women or youths, or anyone not from Ulster. No one dared shed the blood of an Ulsterman in this state. If they did, great turmoil would fall upon them, or else their lives would be cut short.

Twenty-seven warriors came from the islands of Faicha. They broke into the rear of the enclosure as the Ulstermen lay in pain.

The boy-troop were playing in the fields at the time. They heard the women screaming, and immediately ran back, but when they saw the formidable warriors they took flight – all but Cúchulainn. He attacked them with stones and his hurling stick and slew nine of them. The remainder escaped. At this time Cúchulainn was five years of age.

One day Culann the Smith was getting ready to entertain Conchobor and his warriors. He asked Conchobor not to bring too large a force, for he had no land or property to provide for the feast; he only had what he earned with his two hands. Conchobor therefore set out with only fifty of the highest and mightiest of his warriors.

Before he left he visited the playing field. It was his habit to greet the boys and to obtain their blessing. So it was that he saw Cúchulainn playing ball against 150 other boys and beating them. When they played 'shoot-the-goal', the other boys were helpless against him; when they wrestled, he beat the entire 150 of them (there was not room around him for the number needed to beat him); when they played 'the stripping game', he stripped them all stark naked. They could not even pluck the brooch from his cloak. Conchobor was amazed at this and he wondered what Cúchulainn would be like when he reached manhood.

Conchobor invited Cúchulainn to go with him as a guest to the feast Culann the Smith was preparing. Cúchulainn replied that he had not had his fill of play yet, but he said that he would follow on.

Later, when the others had all arrived at the feast, Culann asked Conchobor if there was anyone still to come.

Conchobor said that his foster-son was following.

Culann said he had a fierce hound and three chains were required to hold him back with three men on each chain. The hound was let loose to guard the cattle and other stock, and the gate of the enclosure was shut.

When the boy arrived, the hound came tearing towards him. Cúchulainn had been playing as he came, tossing his ball up and striking it with his hurling stick, then casting his javelin at the ball and catching it before it reached the ground. He never faltered even though the hound was rushing ever nearer.

Conchobor and his men saw the whole thing, but they were too far away to do anything to save the boy.

Cúchulainn continued to play until the very moment the hound sprang. Only then did Cúchulainn set the ball and stick aside. He caught the hound by the throat with one hand and grasped its back with the other. Then he smashed it against the nearest pillar and its limbs leaped from their sockets.

According to another tale, he threw his ball into its mouth with such force that its entrails were torn out.

The Ulstermen rose up to meet him. Some of them clambered over the rampart; others came through the gate of the enclosure. They carried Cúchulainn to Conchobor's bosom, and they gave a great cry of relief that the son of the king's sister had escaped death. Culann said he was welcome for the sake of his mother's heart, but he said that his life would be a waste and his household like a desert without his hound. It had guarded his life and his honour. He said that his hound was a valued servant – a shield and a shelter for their goods and herds. It had guarded all the animals at home and out in the fields.

Cúchulainn said that he himself would be his hound and act as a bodyguard. He said that he would guard all Murtheimne Plain.

No herd or flock would leave his care without him knowing. Cathbad declared that Cúchulainn would be his name – the Hound of Culann. Up until this time, towards the end of his sixth year, Cúchulainn had always been known as Setanta.

Cathbad the Druid was staying with his son, Conchobor mac Nesa. He had 100 men at the ready, learning Druid lore from him. One day a student enquired what that day would be lucky for. Cathbad said that if a warrior took up arms for the first time that day, his name would be known in all of Erin. He would carry out great deeds, and stories about him would live for ever.

Cúchulainn overheard this and immediately went to Conchobor. He said he had come from Cathbad to claim his weapon. Conchobor gave him shield and spear, but there, in the middle of the house, Cúchulainn tested the weapons. Of the fifteen sets Conchobor kept in store for new warriors, or in case of breakages, not one survived. He was given Conchobor's own weapons in the end, and these survived. He made a flourish and saluted their owner, the King. He said that there should be long life to any man who had for his king the man who owned the weapons.

Now Cathbad arrived and noticed that Cúchulainn was fully armed.

Conchobor said, "Was it not by your own direction that he came?"

"Certainly not," said Cathbad.

Conchobor asked Cúchulainn why he lied, and Cúchulainn replied that it was no lie. He said he had heard Cathbad instructing his students one morning south of Emain Macha and he had overheard him saying that whoever armed first would achieve fame and greatness, but his life would be short. Cúchulainn said that he considered this a fair bargain. If he achieved fame he would be content.

On another day Cúchulainn overheard Cathbad talking to another Druid. Cathbad said they stay was also an auspicious one for fame and greatness, so Cúchulainn went to Conchobor and claimed his chariot. It was a repeat of what happened with the weapons. He clasped his hands to the chariot between the shafts, and the frame broke at his touch. In the same way he broke twelve chariots. At last he was given Conchobor's chariot, and that survived.

He mounted the chariot beside Conchobor's charioteer, Ibor by name, and turned it around. Cúchulainn urged Ibor to take the road to the boy-troop, to greet them and obtain their blessing.

After this he asked Ibor to go further up the road, as far as the road would take them.

They arrived at Sliab Fuait and met Conall Cernach there, for to Conall Cernach had fallen the care of the province boundary that day. Any man who came that way was challenged, so no one could slip by Emain Macha without notice. Cúchulainn said that Conall should go back to the fort and let him keep watch for a while, but Conall replied that he was a little young for dealing with men of war and he should stick to poetry. Cúchulainn suggested they should go together to view the shore of Loch Ectra, for warriors were often camped there, and Conall agreed.

As they set off Cúchulainn released a stone from his sling and smashed the shaft of Conall Cernach's chariot.

Conall asked him why he had done this, and Cúchulainn answered, "To test the accuracy of my aim."

Cúchulainn then repeated that Conall should go back to Emain Macha and leave him there to guard alone. In the end Cúchulainn travelled onward alone to Loch Ectra, but he found no one there.

Ibor said to Cúchulainn that they should go back to Emain Macha, where there was the possibility of something to drink, but Cúchulainn said that this was not a good idea.

He pointed towards a peak, and asked Ibor to tell him about it. The charioteer said it was called Sliab Mobdairn, and Cúchulainn asked to be taken there.

When he arrived at the mountain Cúchulainn asked Ibor about the white heap of stones on the mountain top. Ibor said it was a lookout place called the White Cairn. From here Ibor pointed out all the fields, fords, habitations, and other places of note, including every fastness and fortress.

One of these was the fort of the three sons of Nechta Scéne, who were called Foill ('the deceitful'), Fannall ('the swallow') and Tuachell ('the cunning'). Ulli, Lugaid's son, was their father and Nechta Scéne their mother. Ulstermen had killed Ulli and this was the reason why the brothers were enemies of Ulster. They had killed as many Ulstermen as were now living.

Cúchulainn said he would like to be taken to see them, but the charioteer said this would be courting danger. Cúchulainn said he had no wish to avoid danger.

They travelled on and turned their horses loose at a ford to the south and upstream of their enemies' stronghold. Cúchulainn took the spancel-hoop from the pillar-stone at the ford and tossed it as far as he could into the water and let the current take it. When the sons of Nechta Scéne saw the hoop, they knew someone was challenging them and set out to find him. Meanwhile Cúchulainn lay down by the pillar-stone and told Ibor not to wake him if only one man came.

When the sons of Nechta Scéne came up to the ford they learned that their challenger was a little boy out in his chariot for the first time. One of the brothers said the boy's luck had deserted him and that it was a bad beginning in arms for him. Foill told Ibor to get off his land, and graze his horses there no more. Ibor asked the warrior why he should feel enmity for sleeping boy.

Cúchulainn awoke and said he was a boy with a difference – a boy who had come to look for a fight.

"It would be a pleasure," said the warrior.

"You may have that pleasure now, in the ford," Cúchulainn said.

The charioteer told Cúchulainn he should beware of Foill.

"If you fail to cripple him with the first shot, you may thrust away all day."

Cúchulainn flung Conchobor's broad spear and Foill fought no more. It pierced him and broke his back. Cúchulainn killed the next brother, Fannall, with similar skill and efficiency, but there was still Tuachell to overcome, and he had never been beaten in a fight.

Cúchulainn threw the spear at him and tore him apart where he stood.

Cúchulainn cut off the brothers' heads and took them and other trophies back to his chariot. A scream rose up behind them from the mother, Nechta Scéne, as they set out for Emain Macha with all the spoils.

They travelled towards Sliab Fuait, across Breg Plain. The horses overtook the wind and the birds in flight, and Cúchulainn could catch the shot from his sling before it hit the earth.

When they reached Sliab Fuait they came across a herd of deer, and Cúchulainn said he would take back a live deer to surprise the men of Ulster. The charioteer said it was not possible to catch one alive. Cúchulainn said he could, and he instructed the charioteer to drive the horses over the marsh.

The charioteer did so until the horses got bogged down. Then Cúchulainn got out and caught the deer nearest to him. He released the horses from the bog and calmed the deer before tethering it between the rear shafts of the chariot.

Now they saw before them a flock of swans, and Cúchulainn asked if the men of Ulster would prefer some of these to be brought to them dead or alive. The charioteer replied that the quickest way would suffice.

Cúchulainn threw a little stone at the birds and killed eight of them. Then he threw a larger stone and brought down twelve more. He now commanded Ibor to collect the swans, but Ibor could not get out of the chariot. The horses were so mad that he could not get past them; nor could he get over the iron wheels of the chariot, for they were so sharp; nor could he get past the deer, for its antlers filled all the space between the chariot's shafts.

Cúchulainn said to him to step out on to the antlers. He said that he would stare at the deer with such an eye that it would not stir.

When Ibor returned with the swans Cúchulainn pulled the reins, and the chariot gathered up speed. In this way they came back to Emain Macha, with a wild deer behind the chariot, enough swans for a feast, and the heads of Nechta Scéne's three sons.

When he arrived, Cúchulainn turned the left chariot-board towards Emain Macha in insult, and he said that if a man was not found to fight him, he would spill the blood of everyone in the court. He cried out to some naked woman to be sent out to greet him. The women of Emain Macha went forth led by Mugain, the wife of Conchobor mac Nesa, at their head. They bared their breasts at him. Cúchulainn hid his countenance, and immediately the warriors of Emain Macha seized him and plunged him into a vat of cold water, but the vat burst asunder as he lay in it. He was thrust into another vat, this time full of boiling water with bubbles the size of fists. At length he was plunged into a third vat, which was neither too hot or too cold.

Then he stepped out, and Mugain gave him a blue cloak to fit round him with a silver brooch and a hooded tunic. He sat on Conchobor's knee, and that was his seat for ever after.

It was no wonder, Fiacha mac Fir-Febe said, that the warrior who did this in his seventh year would grow to be a great warrior.

Chapter 10

The Stench of Death

At Mag Muceda ('the pig-keeper's plain') Cúchulainn cut down
an oak tree in the path of Ailill's army and cut an ogham message
into the side. He wrote that no one was to pass the oak until a
warrior had leaped in his chariot at the first attempt.

Thirty horses fell trying to leap the tree, and thirty chariots were
smashed, and the place has been called Belach Nane ('the pass
where they drove') ever since.

The next morning, Maeve summoned Fraech mac Fidaig and
said to him, "Go and find Cúchulainn and challenge him."

Early in the morning he went out with nine others, and they
came to where they saw a boy washing in the river. Fraech said
he would attack him in the river, for Cúchulainn was not good in
water. He stripped off his clothes and challenged Cúchulainn in
the river.

Cúchulainn said, "If you come any nearer, I shall have to kill
you, and that will be a pity."

"All the same I shall be coming to meet you in the water, and
you will have to fight," Fraech replied.

"Choose your style of combat," said Cúchulainn.

"Each of us is to keep an arm round the other," Fraech said.

They fought a long time in the water until Fraech went under.
Cúchulainn pulled him up again and said he was willing to spare

him, but Fraech said he would not have it. Cúchulainn thrust him down once again and Fraech died. Ath Fraich was the name of the ford.

His followers carried his body to the camp and the whole company joined hands in lament. A troop of women in green dresses gathered about the body and bore him away into the *síd*. Sid Fraich has been the name of the hill since that time.

Now Fergus leaped in his chariot across the oak tree.

Some say that after they left Ath Fraich they went to Ath Meislir, where Cúchulainn killed six men, including Meslir. Others say they went to Ath Taiten and the six Cúchulainn killed were six Dunglas of Irros.

Now they left for Fornocht ('the naked place').

Maeve had a young hound, and its name was Baiscne. Cúchulainn slung a stone at it and cut off its head, and the place has been called Druin Baiscne ('the ridge of Baiscne') since that time.

Maeve said that it was a shame on them all that they could not destroy this pestering demon that was killing them all. They pursued him until their chariot shafts broke. Next day they travelled across high ground with Cúchulainn ahead of them.

At a place called Támlachtai Orláim, a little to the north of the sanctuary of Disert Lochait, Cúchulainn came upon a charioteer cutting wood. He was Orlám's charioteer, and Orlám was the son of Ailill and Maeve. Some say the shaft of Cúchulainn's own chariot had broken, and he was cutting out a new one when he saw Orlám's charioteer.

Cúchulainn asked him what he was doing there, and the charioteer answered that he was preparing chariot shafts because they had smashed their shafts chasing wild deer.

Cúchulainn said he would do the trimming, and he stripped the shafts through his clenched fist, paring them clean. The charioteer became frightened.

Cúchulainn asked him who he was, and he answered that he was Orlám's charioteer. The charioteer asked Cúchulainn who he was, but Cúchulainn wouldn't tell him. He told him not to worry and asked him where his master was.

The charioteer replied, "Over there at the dyke."

Cúchulainn said he had no quarrel with the charioteers, but he went up to Orlám and beheaded him. Then he shook Orlám's head at the host. He placed the head on the charioteer's back and told him to take it all the way back to his camp. If he disobeyed, he would get a shot from Cúchulainn's sling.

The charioteer returned with the head and told Ailill and Maeve his story.

"This is not like catching birds," she said.

Unfortunately he had met Ailill and Maeve outside the camp, so he took the head off his back there and then, disobeying Cúchulainn's order. Cúchulainn hurled a stone at him, shattering his head, so that his brains were spattered at the ears. It was not true that Cúchulainn did not kill charioteers, but he'd only kill them if they did wrong.

The three sons of Gárach were waiting at the ford that now bears their name – Ath meic Gárach. Their names were Lon ('the blackbird'), Uala ('the prideful') and Diliu ('the torrent'). Their three charioteers were also there, as were their three foster-sons. They planned to kill Cúchulainn and lift the scourge from the army. Three shafts of aspen were cut for their charioteers so that they could all unite against Cúchulainn. This broke the rules of fair combat, but Cúchulainn killed them all.

Now Cúchulainn swore an oath in Methe that from this time onward, whenever he should lay eyes on Maeve and Ailill, he would hurl a slingshot at them. It was following this that he shot a stone across the ford and killed Maeve's squirrel as it sat close to her neck. The place was called Bird Nech Ford ('squirrel-neck ford'). Some say that a bird and a little squirrel were both perched on Maeve's shoulders when their heads were shorn off by slingshots. Also, Rouin was drowned in the lake now called after him.

Ailill said to one of his sons that Cúchulainn could not be far off. The men rose up, looking about them, and as they were settling down again a shot from Cúchulainn's sling struck one of them and shattered his head. Another shot killed Maenén, the jester.

Ailill said that he swore by the gods of his people that he would cut in two any man who derided Cúchulainn. He now urged the party to gather speed, travelling by day and night until they arrived at Cúailnge.

The magical sweet-mouthed men of Cáin came out from under the cataract at Es Ruaid in order to charm the host, but the people thought that they were spies from Ulster who were gathering information. They ran in the shape of deer far ahead of them to the north. They were Druids of great learning.

Lethan stood at the ford on the River Níth in Conaille. He was in a rage about what Cúchulainn had done, and he waited for him. But Cúchulainn severed his head and left it with the body. This ford has been named Ath Lethan since this date. Many chariots were shattered in another ford nearby, and this is still called the Ford of the Chariots. On the shoulder of land that lies between these two fords, Mulca, Lethan's charioteer was killed. It was called Guala Mulchaii ('Mulca's shoulder').

Men were sent continually to their graves.

The Morrígan sat like a bird on a standing stone in Temair Cúailnge, and he asked the brown bull if there would be slaughter, and the bull's prophecy was doom-laden: the wise raven will groan aloud; they will ravage the fields in packs; on the plains there will be war and the cattle will groan. The raven will be ravenous amongst the dead men. There will be war everlasting raging over Cúailnge. There will be death of sons and death of kinsmen. Death! Death!

Thereupon the bull was moved to Sliab Cuilinn with its fifty heifers with the herdsman driving them. It threw off fifty boys who were playing on its back, killing two-thirds of them. It tore up a trench through the land of Marcéni, tossing the earth up with its heels.

In the district of Conaille, beside the dark waters of Saili Imdorchi, Cúchulainn killed no one, but he swore again that whenever he sighted Maeve he would hurl a slingshot at her head. This was not easy to do, for Maeve never went about unless she was protected by half her army, holding a barrel-shaped shelter of shields over their heads.

One day one of Maeve's servants went to fetch water surrounded by a troop of many women. Cúchulainn mistook her for Maeve; he shot two stones at her from Cuinciu and killed her in the place known as Réid Locha, the level ground at Cúailnge.

Chapter 11

From Finnabair in Cúailnge to Conaille

One version of the tale of the brown bull says that the forces divided at Finnabair in Cúailnge and brought them to Conaille. Maeve said that they had not done well enough, for she did not see the bull with him. There was no trace of it anywhere in Ulster, they said.

One of Maeve's herdsmen was summoned, and Maeve asked him where he thought the bull might be. Trembling, the herdsman said that Ulstermen were laid low by their pangs. He said the bull left with all sixty heifers and was now in Dubchoire ('the black cauldron') in Glen Gat ('the glen of the osiers'). Maeve told the herdsmen to catch the bull.

They encircled the bull at Glen Gat and drove it towards Finnabair.

There Cúchulainn attacked Lóthar, one of the herdsmen, with great fury, taking out his entrails. He attacked the camp and the sixty heifers were killed. Fifty warriors also died in this attack. The bull vanished out of the camp.

Maeve asked one of the herdsmen where the bull might be, and she was told that he was back in the fastness of Sliab Cuilinn. They headed towards it, but they could not find the bull there.

In one version of the story, the River Cronn was in spate and they had to pass the night by the edge of the river. In the morning Maeve ordered some warriors to cross it, and the famous warrior Ualu attempted it. He shouldered a heavy flagstone so that the water would not force him backward, but the water overwhelmed him, stone and all. His grave, along with the stone, is on the roadway to the river. Lis Ualonn is its name ('Ualu's flagstone').

At the same place, Cúchulainn killed Cronn and Caendele in a fierce fight. A further hundred warriors perished, including Roan and Roae, the two chroniclers of the Táin. Some say that this was the reason why the tale of Táin was lost. One hundred and twenty kings died by Cúchulainn's hand at the same river.

Maeve and her remaining warriors continued up the River Cronn until they reached its source. They were crossing between the springs and the mountain summit when Maeve decided instead to cross the summit. It took them three days and nights to form the gap of Bernas Bó Cúailnge. They went over it with their chariots and belongings, and they passed the night at Glen Dáilimda in Cúailnge, at the place now called Botha, after the huts were built there. Next day they travelled to the River Colptha, and they tried to make a crossing, but it too rose up against them and carried off the bodies of 100 of their charioteers towards the sea. The Chariot Meadow is the name of the place where they were drowned.

They were forced to move along the River Colptha up to its source and then to Bélat Aliuin. They passed the night between Cúailnge and Conaille at Lisa Liaco, which was so named because the forces built stone shelters for their calves there. After this they travelled on to Glen Gatlach, but the river rose up against them. The river used to be called Sechaire, but it has been known as the River Gatlach since that time. They spent the night at Druim Féne in Conaille.

Other writers of the saga record events differently from the dividing up of the armies at Finnabair to the arrival at Conaille.

When everyone had brought their spoils back to Finnabair Maeve said to divide up the armies. Ailill, she said, should take half of them by the Midluachair road, and she would take the others by way of Bernas Bó Ulad. Fergus said this would leave them with the difficult half of the army, and they would have to cut a gap to get the cattle over the mountain. This is what they did, and such was the origin of the name Bernas Bó Ulad.

At this time Ailill took his charioteer aside and asked him to watch Maeve and Fergus that day. He did not know why they were so intimate and he wanted to know what was going on.

Cuillius found the couple together at Cluithre, where they had lingered before the army moved on. Cuillius moved closer, and the couple did not know he was spying on them. Fergus had taken off his sword and Cuillius was able to draw it out of its sheath and take it back to Ailill as a sign that Fergus and Maeve had been sleeping together. Ailill and Cuillius grinned at each other, and Ailill said Maeve had done it to keep Fergus's help on the Táin. He told Cuillius to place the sword under his chariot seat with some linen around it.

Meanwhile Fergus was looking for his sword. He told Maeve to wait to him while he went into the wood. Maeve did not know his sword had vanished. He left her, taking another sword with him, and cut a wooden sword from a tree. This was how Fid Morthruaille ('the wood of the great scabbard') got its name. Then Fergus went back to his companions.

All the armies met upon the plain and pitched camp. Ailill wanted Fergus to play *fidchell* with him, but when Fergus entered the tent Ailill laughed at him.

There was the prospect of Macha's curse with a quick doom. Galeóin's swords were crying out and the women were unvanquished. There were the leaders of the armies that struggled in fury and men's necks were severed. Ailill asked why he was so wild without his weapons. At a certain ford was his will done. There was much heroism, but an empty shout to Maeve's oaths. There were tribes of men that could bear witness to the struggle with giddy women crawling, entering and battling with great murky deeds under cover everywhere.

Ailill said to sit down and play *fidchell*.

"You have played with a king and queen, ruling the game with eager armies in iron companies all around them. Even if you won," he said, "can you take my place?"

He knew all about kings and queens. He lay first fault straight at the women's own sweet squellings. He loved lust.

Valorous Fergus was coming and going with cattle bellowing, with great forces all over Finnabair's rich places in kingly form with fire of dragon, thrusting out in front. There was Róich's son Fergus, grandson of Rus, the king of kings.

They began their game of *fidchell*, advancing the gold and silver men over the bronze board. Ailill said it was right that death should take the sweet slight king in the coppery point. The mighty Maeve was less secure, as her wise men moved against Fergus.

Maeve said to hold on a while, and not to forget the clownish words, and not to forget what still remained of the gentle boy-troop. A wise judge would bear no grudge, and would have nothing to do with those who keep their cattle with a vengeance. Men's eyes were cast downward and Fergus was cleared.

He said, "We back each other with sharp words in the public eye. But right speech offended, right ways became wrong, and the javelins shot, kings slaying kings."

They stayed there that night, and next morning Ailill spoke out.

There was one warrior facing a large army by the Cronn river, and his deeds were feared by the men of Connaught, and men's blood flowed from hacked necks. Great men met their deaths, and the waves mounted up where the beardless hero came from Ulster.

Maeve said it was wise not to call down violence with chariot onslaughts from rocky heights.

Women were carried off as well as cattle. Swordsmen smashed on either side, and men's deeds of battle shone in the murk. Oxen were driven and women stolen.

At last great armies turned from the battle plain of Cúailnge, and the warriors slept. Fergus stood at the head of the chariot prows, and great heroes would swear by their people. There would be squabbling over queens.

Maeve said, "As you have said, let it be. He bent to your yoke, and hordes were marching, and Ailill's power was put in his hand to some effect."

Now they moved onward as far as the River Cronn. One of Ailill's sons spoke to them and said, "Send out men, for great deeds have to be done. The horned herds should stand fast until he arrived, away from the battlefield. Mighty acts would sweep clean."

Fergus called out to his mighty son not to venture out for he might have his head hacked from his body by the boy with no beard, who had come from the heights.

There were howls on the plain and summons up the rivers that shook the woods. There were mighty acts with men in great numbers that were drowned in the water, and Maeve cried out in mockery. Faces were cast down in the heat of battle.

Fergus asked if he could travel ahead, to make sure there was no foul play against the boy. He said to send the cattle in front and the armies after them, with the women in the rear.

Maeve went on to say that on your soul and oath Fergus should listen and guard the cattle with his armies in a conquering rage. The men of Ulster should halt unless there would be a mighty roar on the plain of Ai. He said that he would meet again on the army's track. Fergus cried out to Maeve to spare them, even though there was shameless talk and harassment. No soft son was ever his at the struggle in Emain Macha. He would strike his people no more blows. He said to let him out from under the great weight, so that no man would come breathing down his neck to do his work on another occasion.

At the ford on the River Cronn Cúchulainn faced them.

"The army is upon us," he said to Laeg, his charioteer.

The charioteer answered that he swore by the gods to do great deeds before these warriors, who would drive in triumph at full speed on slender steeds. They would have yokes of silver and golden wheels to take away kings. His steeds would bring them to victory.

Cúchulainn told Laeg to set a course headlong to crush Macha's great triumph. Let them stray like women on the plain, shaking with terror.

The team's heads were set against Ailill and Maeve. Her two armies were like placid herds grinding amongst them on a vengeful path. Cúchulainn said that he would summon the waters to help him, he would summon earth and air, but above all he would summon the River Cronn. The waters reared up to the treetops.

Now the son of Ailill and Maeve went out before everyone, and Cúchulainn killed him in the ford. Thirty horsemen were overwhelmed with him. Later Cúchulainn slew another thirty-two warriors in the waters. They pitched their tents at this ford, and Lugaid mac Nois Allchomaig went out with thirty horsemen to parley with Cúchulainn.

Cúchulainn bid them welcome. He said that if a flock of wild birds was grazing on the plain he would share them with him. He would stand in the ford in the heat of battle.

Lugaid said that Cúchulainn could hold them off single-handedly. If the army one by one came against them, the Ulster enemy would not forsake him.

Cúchulainn asked if the armies feared him.

Lugaid swore by the gods that they dare not fetch water in ones and twos outside, but they had to go in twenties and thirties.

Cúchulainn said he had something new for them: he was taking up sling-throwing.

Lugaid asked him what he wanted and said Cúchulainn should spare them.

Cúchulainn said he had his promise provided he pointed them out with a sign. He also said to show a sign amongst his men, but they had to swear to watch over his life and send him food every night. At this Lugaid returned, and he found Fergus in Ailill's tent; he called him out and informed him of the news.

Then they heard Ailill cry out: "What are you whispering for, for this is no sports field. For a great army he chooses amongst us for the sake of Róich's son, who was playing king. They heard tell of events and they received great help through Maeve's sweet deeds. They decided to take their few men to the favoured tents, so that all would be safe from flying flagstones and hurtling sods. They knew that he was near.

He swore by the gods that he could not promise without asking the boy again, Lugaid said.

Fergus replied, "Would you do this to me?"

He asked to let him take Ailill and his troop of 3,000 warriors among his own men. Bring an ox, a salt pig and a barrel of wine with him.

Cúchulainn said that it was all the same to him where he goes. So the two troops mingled together and they remained so for the night, or for twenty nights, or thirty, as some have said. Even so Cúchulainn destroyed thirty of Ailill's warriors with his sling. Fergus said that things were becoming worse for the sons of Ulster would soon rise from their pangs, and then they would overcome them. Also, this was a bad place to fight.

Cúchulainn set out towards Cúil Airthir in the east, and he slew thirty warriors at Ath Duirn (the ford of the fist), but they were unable to reach Cúil Airthir until nightfall. Cúchulainn killed thirty more of them before they pitched their tents.

In the morning Ailill's charioteer was washing the bands of his chariot wheels in the ford. Cúchulainn struck him with a stone and killed him. They pushed forward, reaching Druim Féne in Conaille for the night.

This is the second version of how they reached this place.

Chapter 12

Hand-to-Hand Combat

Cúchulainn continued to harass the enemy warriors, and he slew 100 men on each of three consecutive nights, slinging stones at them from the hill called Ochaine nearby.

"At this rate," said Ailill, "our army will fade away at his hands. Take Cúchulainn and offer: I will give him land equal to the whole plain of Murtheimne with the best chariots to be found at Ai and harnesses to equip a dozen men. I will offer him his native plain, with twenty-one bondmaids and compensation for anything of his, such as cattle or household utensils, that has been destroyed."

Ailill even offered to take service under Cúchulainn.

Mac Roth could circle the whole of Ireland in one day, so he was chosen to take the message from Ailill and Maeve. Fergus thought Cúchulainn could be found at Delga.

There was heavy snow that night, and it turned all Ireland into a blanket of white.

Laeg told Cúchulainn a warrior was approaching. The warrior had a linen band around his yellow hair, he held a club, an ivory-hilted sword hung at his waist, and a red-embroidered hooded tunic was wrapped around him.

Cúchulainn asked which of the King's warriors he was.

Laeg answered that he was a dark, good-looking fellow with

a bronze brooch in his attractive brown cloak. He wore a tough triple shirt next to his skin, and a pair of well-woven shoes on his feet. He held a peeled hazel wand in one hand and a single-edged sword with guards of ivory in the other.

Cúchulainn said that these were the marks of a herald.

Cúchulainn was resting haunch-deep in the snow when Mac Roth came up to him and asked him whose servant in arms he was.

Cúchulainn replied that he served Conchobor mac Nesa.

Laeg said, "Can you say nothing clearer than that?"

"It was clear enough," said Cúchulainn.

Mac Roth asked where he could find Cúchulainn, and he revealed the entire message. Cúchulainn would not agree to the terms.

Mac Roth offered him their noblest bondwomen and all the milk cattle out of their plunder if he would stop using his sling against them at night, though he might do as he chose during the days.

Cúchulainn said he could not agree to this.

"If I take away your bondwomen," he said, "your free women will have to resort to the grindstones. If I take away your milk cows, they will have to go without milk." Cúchulainn said the men of Ulster would sleep with their bondwomen and give birth to slavish sons, and they would use the milk cows for meat in the winter.

Mac Roth asked if there was anything that he could offer, and Cúchulainn said there was, but he would not say what it was.

Fergus said he knew what Cúchulainn had in mind and that it boded him no good. He outlined his plan: that he would fight them one by one in the ford, and that no cattle should be taken from the ford for a day and a night after each fight. This plan would gain time for him until help arrived from the men of Ulster. Fergus said they were so long recovering from their pangs.

Ailill said it would be easier on them to lose one man every day than 100 every night.

Fergus went to Cúchulainn with the proposal, and he was followed by Etarcomol, son of Eda and Léthrenn, a foster-son of Ailill and Maeve. Fergus said he would rather Etarcomol did not come, for fear of ill feeling between him and Cúchulainn. He thought no good could come of the meeting.

Etarcomol said he would like to be under Fergus's protection.

"Yes," said Fergus, "but only if you do not insult Cúchulainn."

They went to Delga in two chariots, and when they arrived Cúchulainn happened to be playing *buannach* with Laeg. Cúchulainn was facing away from them and Laeg was facing towards them. Laeg saw two chariots coming. In the first chariot there was a great dark man, his hair dark and full. A purple cloak was wrapped around him, held by a gold brooch. He wore a red-embroidered hooded tunic. He carried a curved shield with an edge of gold and a stabbing spear. There was a sword as large as a boat's rudder at his thigh.

"It is a big empty rudder," said Cúchulainn. "That is my friend, Fergus, and it is not a sword but a stick he has in his scabbard."

Fergus came up, and Cúchulainn welcomed him as a friend. He said that if the salmon were swimming in the rivers, he would give him one and share another. If wild birds were to settle on the plain, he would give him one and share another. A drink would be available out of the sands. He would be present at the ford where there would be a fight. He would be watching while he slept.

Fergus believed him, but he said it wasn't food they came for.

Then Cúchulainn heard Fergus's message, after which Fergus left.

Etarcomol remained, staring at Cúchulainn, and Cúchulainn asked him what he was staring at.

Etarcomol said, "I am staring at you."

"You could take that in at a glance," Cúchulainn said.

Etarcomol said he saw nothing to be afraid of – no cause for the terror of the multitudes. He said Cúchulainn seemed to be a fine lad who performed graceful tricks with wooden weapons.

Cúchulainn said Etarcomol was belittling him, but for Fergus's sake he would not kill him. If he had not had Fergus's protection, he would have had his bowels ripped out by now and his quarters scattered behind him all the way from his chariot to the camp.

"You need not threaten me any more," said Etarcomol, and he added that he would be the first of the men of Erin to come against him.

At this he left. He said to his charioteer that he had sworn in front of Fergus to fight Cúchulainn the following day, but he would not wait. He said to turn the horses round from the hill again.

Laeg saw this and warned Cúchulainn that the chariot was coming back. He noticed that Etarcomol had turned the left chariot board as an insult.

They met at the ford and Cúchulainn cut the sod from underneath Etarcomol's feet so that he fell flat with the sod on his stomach.

Cúchulainn said, "Now go away. I would have cut you to pieces long ago if it was not for Fergus."

Etarcomol said he would have his head.

Cúchulainn slashed at Etarcomol's armpits with his sword, and his clothes fell away leaving the skin untouched. Cúchulainn again ordered him to leave, but still Etarcomol refused. Now Cúchulainn cut off his hair with his sword, as close as a razor, leaving the skin unscathed. Still Etarcomol persisted, so Cúchulainn split his head open.

Fergus saw Etarcomol's chariot passing by him with only one man in it and he returned to Cúchulainn in a fury.

Cúchulainn told Fergus not to rage at him, and reminded him that he had run from Ulster without his sword. He said he honoured mighty warriors, but Etarcomol had menaced him, so he had died. He told his friend Fergus not to fret. He stooped humbly while Fergus's chariot circled him three times.

Etarcomol's charioteer averred that Cúchulainn was not at fault, as Etarcomol had sworn he would not leave until he had his head.

Fergus pierced Etarcomol's heels with a spancel-ring and dragged him behind his chariot back to the camp. As they were travelling over rocky ground the body split into halves.

When Maeve saw this, she said it was brutal treatment for the unfortunate dog.

Fergus replied that he was an arrogant whelp to dare pick a fight with the great Hound of Culann.

They dug a grave for him, and his name was written in ogham on his gravestone.

Cúchulainn killed no more warriors that night.

Lugaid now said, "What men do we have to attack Cúchulainn tomorrow?"

One of Ailill's sons said they could find no more than one warrior to attack him.

Maeve said, " Ask him for a truce while we look for others."

"But where can we turn to," Ailill asked, "to find an adversary for Cúchulainn, for he has no match in Ireland?"

Cúroi would not come because he thought he had done enough in sending his men.

A message was sent to Nadcranntail, and Maine Andoe ('the swift one') was the messenger. Nadcranntail said he would not fight unless he could have Maeve's daughter Finnabair. He went back with Andoe, and his weapons were carried in a wagon from the east of Connaught to the camp. Maeve said that he could have Finnabair if he went against Cúchulainn, so Nadcranntail agreed.

Lugaid warned Cúchulainn that Nadcranntail would be attacking the following day, and that he would not be able to resist him. Cúchulainn said that he would see.

Nadcranntail left the camp next morning and took nine spears of holly with him, charred and sharpened. Cúchulainn was there before him in the distance catching birds. His chariot was nearby. Nadcranntail let fly a spear at Cúchulainn, who toyed in mid-air with the point of this spear, and his bird-catching never faltered. He did the same with the next eight spears Nadcranntail threw at him. When the ninth spear was flung the birds flew away from Cúchulainn and he sped off in pursuit. Bird-like, Cúchulainn stepped from point to point of the flying spears in his hurry not to let the birds escape. However, to most people watching Cúchulainn appeared to be running away from Nadcranntail.

Maeve said a true warrior had come and a cowardly spirit had vanished.

Fergus and his men of Ulster were worried about this, and Fiacha mac Fir-Febe protested to Cúchulainn. Fergus said he ought to have stood and shown his bravery, but now it would be better to hide. He had shamed Ulster as well as himself.

Cúchulainn asked who was boasting about putting him to flight, and Fiacha said it was Nadcranntail. Cúchulainn said Nadcranntail had nothing to boast about, and the feat he had performed before them was nothing to be ashamed of. If Nadcranntail had been carrying real weapons, he would not be boasting now, but Cúchulainn did not kill unarmed men.

"Let him come tomorrow between Ochaine and the sea. There he will find me waiting patiently and there will be no question of flight," Cúchulainn said.

Cúchulainn went to this meeting place and kept watch through the night. In the morning he covered himself with a cloak. There was a large stone standing near the place, as big as himself. Nadcranntail arrived with his weapons in the wagon.

Nadcranntail said, "He seems different from yesterday. Is he really Cúchulainn?"

Cúchulainn said, "What if I am?"

Nadcranntail said he could not behead a harmless boy.

Cúchulainn said that he was not the real Cúchulainn, but he would find him behind the hill.

Cúchulainn realised that Nadcranntail would refuse to fight unless he had a beard, so he put on a false one and went to meet Nadcranntail again.

Nadcranntail wanted to fight with rules, and the rules he chose were that they were to throw spears in turn, but there was to be no dodging. Cúchulainn agreed.

Nadcranntail made the first cast, but Cúchulainn leaped

upwards. The spear struck the standing stone, shattering it in two.

Nadcranntail said Cúchulainn had fought foul: he had dodged his throw, but Cúchulainn said he was free to dodge by leaping upwards.

Now it was Cúchulainn's turn. He threw his spear so high that it dropped down into Nadcranntail's skull and pinned him to the earth.

Nadcranntail cried out, "Misery! Misery!"

He said that Cúchulainn was the best warrior in Ireland, and then he said he had twenty-four sons in the camp, and he asked Cúchulainn to let him go and tell them about the treasure he had hidden. He agreed to come back to be beheaded. If the spear was taken out of his head, he would die. Cúchulainn agreed.

Nadcranntail made his way back to the camp, and the others asked him where Cúchulainn's head was. He said they would have to wait. First he had things to tell his sons; then he would go back to fight with Cúchulainn.

After a while he went after Cúchulainn again and flung his sword at him, but Cúchulainn leaped into the air and the sword went harmlessly by. Cúchulainn swelled with fury as he did when he faced the boy-troop at Emain Macha long before. Nadcranntail sprang on to the rim of Cúchulainn's shield, trying to cut his head off, but Cúchulainn struck Nadcranntail again, this time through the neck down to the navel, so he fell in four sections to the ground.

Cúchulainn sang out that Nadcranntail was no more.

Chapter 13

The Bull Is Found

Now with a third of her force Maeve set out into the district of Cuib to look for the bull. Cúchulainn followed. She had planned to lay waste the lands of the Ulstermen and the Picts along the Midlauchair, raiding northwards as far as Dún Sobairche.

Cúchulainn caught sight of Buide mac Báin at the head of sixty of Ailill's men. They were all dressed in cloaks, coming from the direction of Sliab Cuilinn, and they had the brown bull with them surrounded by fifteen heifers. Cúchulainn approached them and asked where they got the cattle.

"From that mountain there," the leader said.

Cúchulainn went to the ford after them in three great strides and spoke again. He asked the leader what his name was.

He replied, "One who neither fears nor favours you – Buide mac Báin.

Cúchulainn said, "Here is a spear for you," and he tossed it through his armpit, severing his liver in two with the spear point. The ford became known as Ath Buide, after the man who was killed there.

It was said at this time that Cúchulainn would be less troublesome if his javelin was taken from him. Ailill's satirist, Redg, was sent to get the javelin from him; but when he asked for the javelin as a gift, Cúchulainn said he would give him any gift but that.

"Other gifts I do not want," replied Redg.

Cúchulainn struck him for refusing the offer.

Redg said he would deprive Cúchulainn of his good name if he did not obtain the javelin.

Cúchulainn flung the javelin at him for refusing what he had offered, and it shot through his head. Redg cried out that it was a stunning gift. In this way Ath Tolam Set got its name ('the ford of the overwhelming gift'). The point of the javelin came to rest at a ford further east, and the name Umsrrith ('where the copper came to rest') was given to that ford.

Cúchulainn killed a number of warriors in Cuib. Then he turned again towards Murtheimne Plain to defend his home. He killed the men of Cronech at Focherd, where he found them pitching tents – the ten cup-bearers and the ten warriors.

Maeve turned back again from the North after spending two weeks harassing Ulster. She had attacked Finnmór, the wife of Celtchar mac Uthidir. She had taken fifty women from her at the capture of Dún Sobairche, in the kingdom of the Dál Riata. Where Maeve rested her horsewhip in the territory of Cuib, the name Bile Mebda ('Maeve's whip') has remained. Other places where Maeve stopped became known as Maeve's Ford, Maeve's Hill and so on.

They all met again at Focherd – Ailill and Maeve and the troop that drove the bull. The herdsman who had been captured with the bull tried to make off with it, but they drove the herd after him into a narrow gap by beating their spear shafts on their shields. The animals' hoofs drove him into the soil. Forgaimen was the herdsman's name.

Cúr mac Dalath was the next warrior to fight Cúchulainn. Maeve said that if he killed Cúchulainn, she and her followers would win.

"It should take a great burden off the army," she said.

Cúr got up, but he drew back when he saw the beardless Cúchulainn, just a boy, opposing him. He said that it was unfitting for a warrior to fight a boy.

Cúchulainn was trying his special feats of arms – the apple-feat, the feats of the sword-edge and the sloped shield, the feats of the javelin and rope, the body feat, the feat of cat and the salmon leap, the pole-throw and the leap over a poisoned stake, the noble chariot-fighter's crouch, the feat of the chariot wheel, the feat of the shield rim, the breath feat, the hero's scream; the stroke of precision, the stunning shot, and stepping on a lance in flight.

The first third of the day, Cúr attacked Cúchulainn from the shelter of his shield, but he could not touch him with a thrust or cast. Cúchulainn was intent upon his feats and did not know that anyone was attacking him until Fiacha mac Fir-Febe warned him to watch out for the man attacking him. Cúchulainn looked about him and flung the one apple left in his hand. It flew between the shield-rim and frame and broke out through the back of Cúr's head.

Now Fergus went back along the road to the armies. He said that they were bound by their pact to wait another day. Ailill said they should go back to their tents.

Láth mac Dabró was asked, like Cúr, to attack Cúchulainn, and he too fell. Foirc mac trí n-Aignech was another of those killed in single combat with Cúchulainn.

Cúchulainn said to Laeg, "Go to the camp and ask Lugaid mac Nois Allchomaig who is to fight me tomorrow."

Lugaid told Laeg that Cúchulainn was luckless – one man against the men of Ireland.

"Ferbaeth will go against Cúchulainn tomorrow," he said, "and may his weapons be cursed!"

They had promised him kingship over his people.

Laeg returned to Cúchulainn, who said that Laeg did not seem very happy with the answer. Laeg told him the news: Ferbaeth had been called to Ailill and Maeve's tent and told to sit at Finnabair's side. He had been told that he was to have her, and that she had picked him to fight Cúchulainn. They called him their man of strength because he had had the same training with Scáthach as Cúchulainn had. They plied him with wine until he became drunk. Although Ferbaeth was Cúchulainn's foster-brother and sworn to him for ever, he was determined to meet him and cut his head off.

Cúchulainn sent Laeg to ask Lugaid to come to talk with him, to which Lugaid agreed.

"It will be a black day," Cúchulainn said. "He will not live to see its end."

They were equal in age and alertness, so they were a perfect match.

"It will be false heroism to oppose me," said Cúchulainn. "Ask him to come and talk with me tonight."

Lugaid passed on the message and Ferbaeth agreed. He said he would go with Fiacha mac Fir-Febe to end his friendship with Cúchulainn. Cúchulainn begged him by their foster-brotherhood and by their common foster-nurse, Scáthach, not to fight.

Ferbaeth said he could not back down for he had made a promise to Maeve.

Cúchulainn left him in a bad temper.

In the glen a piece of split holly drove into Cúchulainn's foot and the point came out at his knee; but he pulled it out.

Ferbaeth said, "Throw it over here," and Cúchulainn did so.

It pierced the back of his head and came out at his mouth, so that he fell backwards in the glen. Ferbaeth exclaimed that it was a great throw. Some say this was the reason the place got its name – the Place of the Throw – and the glen became known as Ferbaeth's Glen.

Fergus was heard singing at Cúchulainn's victory.

"Your comrade has fallen," he said.

Cúchulainn sent Laeg to find out if Ferbaeth was still alive, but Lugaid said that Ferbaeth was dead.

"Someone else will have to meet him tomorrow," Lugaid said.

Ailill said, "I will back no one unless he uses trickery. Give wine to anyone that comes, for it will give him courage, and tell him it is the last wine I took from Cruachan. I would not like them to drink water in the camp. Put Finnabair at your right hand and say that she will be given to anyone who brings me the head of the Warped One."

Each night a great warrior took up the challenge, but one by one they were slain. Eventually, no one could be found to fight him.

They turned to Láréne mac Nois, brother of the King of Munster, and a vainglorious man. They gave him wine and placed Finnabair at his right hand. Maeve said they were a handsome couple and they would make a fine match.

Ailill said, "Fair enough!" and he agreed that Láréne could have her if he brought him the head of the Warped One.

Láréne said he would bring it.

Lugaid went to speak with Cúchulainn at Ferbaeth's Glen.

Lugaid said that he was there to talk about Láréne, his fool of a brother. They had tricked him with the same girl. For the sake of their friendship he begged Cúchulainn not to kill him and leave him brotherless, but he did not mind if he severely punished him, for he was coming against Lugaid's wishes.

Next day Láréne went out to meet Cúchulainn with the girl beside him urging him on. Cúchulainn attacked him and took away his weapons. He caught him in his two hands and shook him until the dung had been forced out of him. The ford grew foul with the smell. In every direction the air thickened with dust. Then Cúchulainn thrust him into Finnabair's arms.

Láréne could not empty his bowels when he wished. He was never free from chest pains, and he could not eat without groaning. He was the only man that had escaped Cúchulainn with his life on the Táin Bó Cúailnge. But it was a cruel escape.

Cúchulainn now saw a young woman of pleasant figure coming towards him wrapped in garments of many colours, and he asked who she was. She said she was King Buan's daughter. She had brought treasure and cattle. She told Cúchulainn she loved him because of the great tales she had heard. Cúchulainn said she had come at a bad time – he could not please a woman while he was in his present circumstances. She said that she might be of help. He said that it was not for a woman that he underwent this ordeal. She said that when the fight was at its peak she would come to his aid.

She threatened to get under his feet like an eel and trip him in the ford. Cúchulainn said this was easy to believe, but that she was no king's daughter. He said he would crack her eel's ribs with his toes and she would carry that stigma for ever unless he lifted it with his blessing.

She threatened to come in the shape of a grey she-wolf, to stampede the beasts into the ford against him. He said he would hurl a slingshot at her and burst the eye in her head and she would carry the mark for ever unless he lifted the curse from her with his blessing.

She threatened to come in the shape of a hornless red heifer and lead the cattle herd to trample him in the waters. He said he would hurl a stone at her and break her leg.

At this she left him.

Lóch mac Mofemis was asked to fight Cúchulainn. He was promised a part of the fine plain of Ai equal to the plain of Murtheimne, with harnesses for a dozen warriors and a chariot worth seven bondmaids. But he did not like the idea of fighting with a boy.

Lóch had a brother called Long, and to him in turn they offered a similar reward – the girl, the harnesses, the chariot and the land.

Cúchulainn killed him, and his body was carried back to his brother. Lóch said that if he could be sure it was a grown man that had killed him, he would seek vengeance.

The women called out to Cúchulainn that those who came were mocking him because he had no beard. Only reckless men and not prime warriors would fight him. They advised him to make a beard with berry juice if he wanted Lóch to fight him.

He took their advice and gave himself a convincing artificial beard.

The women said, "Look – Cúchulainn has a beard!"

They did this to urge Lóch on, but Lóch said that he would not fight him for seven days. Maeve said that they could not leave Cúchulainn in peace for so long, and a warrior was sent every night to steal up and catch him off guard. Cúchulainn killed them all.

Maeve taunted Lóch: "It is a great shame", she said, "that the man who killed your brother should destroy the forces and you still have not gone to fight him. Surely an overgrown elf like you can resist the force of a warrior like Cúchulainn, for was it not from the same teacher that you both learned your skills?"

Lóch went out to avenge his brother. He was satisfied that he would be fighting a bearded man. Lóch said to come to the ford upstream, for he did not want to fight him in the place where Long fell.

As Cúchulainn was making for the ford, men drove some cattle over it.

Gabrán, the poet, said, "There will be great trampling in the river today."

The men fought each other at the ford. As they were in the thick of the fight an eel flung three coils about Cúchulainn's feet and he fell into the water. Lóch immediately set upon Cúchulainn with his sword until the water was blood-red.

Fergus cried out to put heart into Cúchulainn for he feared he might die for want of encouragement. Bricriu mac Carbad started to taunt Cúchulainn.

"Your strength is withered up," he said. "If a little salmon can reduce you like this, the men of Ulster will rise up. If this is what happens when you meet a tough warrior, it is a pity you ever took on a hero's task with all the men of Ireland looking on."

Cúchulainn rose up at this. He struck the eel and smashed its ribs.

A she-wolf appeared and began driving some cattle into the ford, but Cúchulainn let fly with a stone from his sling and burst the eye in the wolf's head.

Then a hornless red heifer appeared and led the cattle thundering into the ford. Cúchulainn cried out, and he could not tell the water for the blood, but he flung a stone at the heifer and broke its legs.

The Morrígan had come in three guises as she had threatened

to do and he had defeated her. At this point he began to sing. He sang that he was alone against the hordes, and that he could neither halt nor pass; he appealed for Conchobor to come now and that it would not be too soon.

"Mágach's sons have stolen our cattle to share between them."

Cúchulainn had held them single-handedly, but one stick would not make fire – give him two or three sticks and he would make fire. He was worn out by single combat. He could not kill all their best warriors alone.

He returned to the fight with Lóch using the sword with the *gae bolga* that his charioteer had given him. Eventually he drove it into Lóch's body and Lóch fell forward on his face. This place has been named Tír Mór ('the ford of yielding'). Now Cúchulainn cut off his head.

A great tiredness now fell upon Cúchulainn, and the Morrígan appeared to him in the guise of a squint-eyed old woman, milking a cow with three teats. He asked her for a drink, and she gave him milk from the first teat.

Cúchulainn said, "Good health to the giver, and may the blessing of the gods be upon her."

Then she gave him milk from the second teat and her eye was made whole. Then she gave him milk from the third teat and her legs were made whole.

The Morrígan had said that she would never heal him.

Chapter 14

Great Death

Ailill and Maeve sent Lugaid to ask Cúchulainn for a truce, but Cúchulainn told him to have a man at the ford the following day. Now, there were six pairs of soldiers of royal blood in Maeve's army – six sons of the kings of the Clanna Dedad. They were known as the Three Dark-Haired Ones of Imlech and the Three Redheads of Sruthar.

They said, "Why should we not go together to fight Cúchulainn?"

So they attacked him the next day and Cúchulainn killed all six.

Maeve considered once again what she could do with Cúchulainn, for she was greatly worried about the number of her warriors Cúchulainn had killed. She decided to ask him to meet with her in a certain place and then to send a great number of warriors against him. She sent her messenger with a false offer of peace. She told him to come unarmed and she said she would have only her troop of women in attendance. Cúchulainn agreed.

Laeg ask Cúchulainn how he planned to go to this meeting with Maeve.

"The way Maeve asked me," said Cúchulainn.

The charioteer said Maeve was a forceful woman, not to be caught off guard. A warrior without his weapons was not governed by the law; he would be treated like a coward.

Cúchulainn took heed of what he had said.

The rendezvous was on a hill known as Ard Aighnech, now called Focherd. Maeve arrived there and set a trap for Cúchulainn with fourteen of her best warriors. When Cúchulainn arrived at the meeting place the men attacked him. Fourteen javelins were thrust at him, but Cúchulainn guarded himself so that his skin was not touched. He turned on them, killing all fourteen of them. They are remembered as the Warriors of Cronech for it was at Cronech near Focherd that they died.

Cúchulainn sang again. He sang that his skill in arms was growing mighty; on fine armies he had laid famous blows; he waged war upon the whole hosts to crush their heroic chiefs, along with Maeve and Ailill, who stirred up wrongs and marched in treachery. Some believe the name *Focherd* comes from the opening words of the chant. Cúchulainn was a fierce, right-speaking warrior full of noble deeds. He fell upon the army as they were setting up camp, killing more warriors. Afterwards, on the same day, they again fought him foul. Five warriors attacked him together, but Cúchulainn killed them single-handedly.

Fergus said they must stop breaking the rules of fair play against Cúchulainn, and they reverted to single combat. Cúchulainn slew Fota in the field now called after him; he slew Bómailce on his ford; Salach in his marsh; Muinne on his hill; Luair in Lethbera; and Fertóithle in Toithle. These places were for ever named after the men who died there. Cúchulainn slew many other important warriors, and Maeve said it was a crime to kill so many of her people. From this time comes the name of Glais Chrau ('the stream of blood') and the ford of Cét Chuile.

Cúchulainn pelted his enemies from his position at Delga, which is now called Dún Cinn Coros, and eventually no living beast would show itself between Delga and the sea.

Lugaid took a message from Ailill to Cúchulainn saying he could have Finnabair if he left their armies alone, but Cúchulainn said he did not trust Ailill.

"It is the word of a king. It is no lie," Lugaid replied.

Cúchulainn said he would accept, so Lugaid took Cúchulainn's reply back to Maeve and Ailill.

Ailill had the camp fool made up to look like him, with a king's crown on his head. He was told to stand at a distance from Cúchulainn so as not to be recognised, and the girl was sent along with him. Ailill told the fool he could marry her to Cúchulainn and then come away quickly.

"The trick might hold him back until the day he should come with the men of Ulster to the last battle," Ailill said.

The fool, Tamun ('the stump'), was sent with the girl. He spoke from a distance with Cúchulainn, but Cúchulainn realised by his tone of voice that he was a fool. He shot a sling-stone, which hit the fool's head, knocking out his brains.

Cúchulainn approached the girl, and thrust a pillar-stone under her tunic. He thrust another pillar-stone up the fool's backside. The two standing stones are still there, Finnabair's Pillar-Stone and the Fool's Pillar-Stone. Cúchulainn left them in this condition.

Some of Ailill's and Maeve's warriors went to look for them because they had stayed away so long, and soon the story spread throughout the entire encampment. There was no possibility of a truce with Cúchulainn after that.

The armies of the four provinces of Erin now camped on Murtheimne Plain, at Breslech Mór ('the place of the great carnage'). They sent their cattle and plunder southwards ahead of them to Clithar Bó Ulad ('the cattle shelter of Ulster'). Cúchulainn took up his place near them at the grave mound in Lerga.

At nightfall Cúchulainn's charioteer kindled a fire for him. He saw in the distance the flickering of gold weapons in the sunset. Fury seized him when he saw the army. He shook his shield and rattled his spears. He brandished his sword and cried out from his throat. The demons and devils and goblins of the countryside replied, so loud was the call.

Nemain stirred up the armies into confusion, and the weapons of the four provinces of Erin shook with fear. One hundred warriors fled in fright that night in the heart of their guarded camp.

Laeg saw a lone man crossing between the camp of the men of Erin towards him from the north-east. He warned Cúchulainn, who asked what sort of man he was. He was a broad man, and his hair was close-cropped, blond and curled. He wore a green cloak, held at his breast by a silver brooch. He wore a kingly tunic of silk embroidered in red gold, and he had white skin. There was a touch of light gold on his black shield. He carried a five-pointed spear in his hand and a forked javelin. His feats were awe-inspiring, but no one was taking notice of him and he heeded no one. It was as if he could not see them.

Cúchulainn guessed that one of his enemies had taken pity upon him, alone on the Táin Bó Cúailnge against all the provinces of Erin.

He was right. The warrior had come to help him, and Cúchulainn asked him who he was. He replied that he was Lug mac Ethnenn.

Cúchulainn said that his wounds were great, and it was time for them to heal, and Lug suggested that he should sleep for three days and three nights by the grave mound at Lerga while he stood against the armies in his place. He sang to Cúchulainn until he went to sleep. He then examine each wound and cleaned it.

Lug started to sing: "Rise up, sons of Ulster, with healed wounds; a fair man faces your enemies in the long night over the ford; everywhere hosts would be defeated, and succour had come to him in this place; a boy was left on guard defending the cattle; he would kill ghosts while he lived; they had none to match his force and temper; when chariots travelled the valleys it was time to rise up.

Cúchulainn slept the three days and nights. From the Monday after the feast of Samhain at the end of summer to the Wednesday after the feast of Imbolc at the beginning of spring, Cúchulainn had never slept, except perhaps against his spear for a moment after midday. He wanted to hack and hew and smite and slaughter the armies of the four great provinces of Erin.

Lug dropped herbs and grasses into Cúchulainn's sore wounds so that he started to recover in his sleep without knowing it.

At this time the boy-troop in Ulster spoke amongst themselves. They said it was terrible that Cúchulainn, their friend, should have to do without help.

"Let us send a company to help him," Fiachna Fuilech ('the bloodspiller') said.

The boy-troop came down from Emain Macha in the north carrying their hurling sticks – three times fifty sons of Ulster kings. They made up a third of the whole troop, led by Follamain, Conchobor's son.

The army spotted them marching over the plain, and Fergus went out to look.

Ailill was afraid that if they joined up with Cúchulainn it would not be possible to stand against them, so he sent 150 warriors to confront them.

They all died at one another's hands at Lia Toll ('the pierced standing stone'). The only survivor from the boy-troop was Follamain mac Conchobor.

Follamain swore he would never return to Emain Macha without Ailill's head with a gold crown on top. This was no easy thing to accomplish.

The two sons of Ailill's foster-mother and foster-father died too.

Ailill was in a hurry to move on while Cúchulainn was out of action. There would be no forcing past him once he sprang from his sleep.

When he awoke, Cúchulainn passed his hands across his face and turned crimson from head to foot with great excitement. He was in good spirits and felt fit for a festival, or for marching or mating. He felt ready for a drink.

Cúchulainn cried out, "How long have I been in this deep sleep?"

Lug said, "Three days and three nights."

Cúchulainn said, "Alas for that!"

"Why?" Lug asked.

Cúchulainn demanded to know what had happened while he was asleep and Lug told him that the boy-troop had come south from Emain Macha – 150 warriors, sons of Ulster kings, led by Follamain, Conchobor's son.

"They fought three battles with the armies of Erin in three days and nights," Lug said, "and all the boy-troop were killed except Follamain mac Conchobor. Follamain swore he would cut off Ailill's head, but he failed and he too was killed.

Cúchulainn cried out that if he had had the strength, the boy-

93

troop would not have perished and Follamain mac Conchobor would not have died.

Cúchulainn said there was no stain on his good name, no question of his courage. He asked Lug to stay with him that night, so that they could avenge the boy-troop together, but Lug said he would not stay. No matter what great deeds a man performed in Cúchulainn's company, the glory would be his. Lug encouraged Cúchulainn and said he could go alone against the armies.

Cúchulainn was anxious to know from Laeg if his second chariot could be yoked. The charioteer donned his skin tunic of stitched deer's leather, light, supple and smooth. He put this on over a feathery outer garment made, some said, by the King of the Romans and given by him to Conchobor, and by Conchobor to Cúchulainn, and by Cúchulainn to Laeg. Then Laeg put on his battle-cap, rich in colour and shape. It suited him well and was no burden. To set him apart from his master, he placed the charioteer's sign on his brow – a single red-gold strip of burning gold, shaped on an anvil's edge. He took the long horse-spancel and the ornamental goad in his right hand. In his left hand he grasped the steed-ruling reins that gave the charioteer control.

Cúchulainn threw the decorated iron armour over the horses, covering them from head to foot with spears, blades and barbs. Every inch of the chariot shone, every angle and corner, front and rear. He cast a spell on his horses, making them obscure to all the camp. Meanwhile everything remained clear to them. It was as well that he cast this spell for he needed the skills of his charioteer that day for leaping gaps and steering straight.

The hero Cúchulainn, Sualdam's son, builder of Badb's fold with walls of human bodies, seized the warrior's battle-harness. It was made up of twenty-seven tunics of waxed skin, pressed together and fastened with strings and cord. He wore it against his clear skin, so that his brain would not burst with the onset of his fury. Over this he put on his battle-belt of tanned leather from the choicest of the hides of seven yearlings, covering him from his armpits. He wore this to repel shots from javelins, lances and arrows. They fell from him as though dashed against a rock. Now he drew on his silk apron with its light gold-speckled leather from the choicest parts of the hides of four yearlings, with a belt of cowhide to hold it.

Then Cúchulainn gripped his weapons: eight short swords, including his flashing ivory-hilted sword; eight small spears, including his five-pronged spear; a quiver; eight light javelins, including his ivory javelin; eight small darts, including his feat-playing dart, the *del chliss*; eight feat-playing shields, including a dark-coloured shield that could hold a prize boar in its hollow. Its entire rim was razor-sharp so it could split a single hair. When Cúchulainn performed the feat of the shield he could fight with his shield as sharply as with a spear or sword. He placed upon his head his crested battle-helmet.

In every nook and cranny his long-drawn scream re-echoed like the cries of 100 warriors. So it was that the demons of the glen cried out from above and around him whenever he went into battle. His cloak was spread about him, made from cloth from Tír Tairngire ('the land of promise'), which was given to him by his magical foster-father.

Cúchulainn had become a monstrous being, hideous and shapeless, and unheard of. His joints, every knuckle and angle, and every organ from his head to his feet shook like a tree in the flood of a stream. His body made a furious twist inside his skin, so that his feet and shins and knees twisted. The balled sinews of his calves switched to the front of his shins. His heels and calves switched. Each big knot of muscle was the size of a great warrior's fist. On his head the sinews of his temple stretched to his neck, each mighty knob as big as the head of a month-old child. His face and features became red, and he sucked one eye so deeply into his head that a wild crane could not place it on to his cheeks from his skull. The other eye fell out and lay on his cheek. His mouth became distorted, and his cheeks peeled back from his jaws and his gullet was visible. His lungs and liver flapped in his mouth and throat. Mists and spurts of fire flickered red in the vaporous clouds that rose boiling above his head, so great was his temper. The hair on his head twisted like a tangle of a red thorn bush. If a royal apple tree with all its kingly fruit were shaken above him, not an apple would fall on the ground, but each would be spiked upon the bristle of his hair as it stood upon his head in rage. The hero-halo rose out of his brow, long and broad as a warrior's whetstone, long as a snout.

He rattled his shields, urging on the charioteer and harassing the hosts.

When the spasm had run its course through the hero Cúchulainn, he stepped into his chariot, which glistened with blades, hooks, prongs and spikes, with ferocious instruments and tearing nails on its shaft. The body of the chariot was slight but erect, with space for a warrior's weapons, swift as the wind or a swallow, or a deer running over the level plain.

The chariot was drawn by two fast steeds, wild and wicked, neat-headed and narrow-bodied, firm in hoof and harness. One horse was swift on foot, high-arched and powerful, with great hoofs. The other, also swift, had a flowing mane.

Cúchulainn drove out to meet his foes. He performed his thunder-feat, killing 100, then 200, then 300, then 400, then 500. He did not think it was necessary to kill many in the first attack, and this was his first important battle with the provinces of Erin.

He circled the enemy in his chariot and he attacked them in hatred. So deeply did his chariot wheels sink into the earth that boulders were torn up as he circled them. A barrier of earth and stones was thrown up about the armies of the four great provinces to prevent them from fleeing. He had them trapped where he could wreak vengeance upon them for the boy-troop.

He went into the middle of them and mowed down the enemy. They fell sole to sole and neck to headless neck. Great was the destruction.

He circled them in the chariot three times, and left a bed of corpses six-deep in a great circuit.

This carnage became known as the Sicfold ('slaughter'). It is one of three slaughters in the Táin. The death toll was unknown, and unknowable, but only the chiefs had been counted. Cúchulainn slew 130 kings as well as an uncountable number of dogs and horses, women and children, and other rabble. Not one man in three escaped unhurt.

When the battle was over Cúchulainn was left without a scratch or a stain on himself, his charioteer or his horses.

Chapter 15

An Important Contest

Next morning Cúchulainn came out to review the armies, and to display his warlike figure to the matrons and virgins, to the young girls, poets and bards. He preferred to display himself by day because he felt that the unearthly shape he had shown them the night before had not done him justice. Certainly the young Cúchulainn was handsome as he came to show himself to the forces. He had three distinct heads of hair, brown at the base, blood-red in the middle and a crown of golden yellow. His hair hung down in glowing splendour over his shoulders, beautiful and fine as gold. The red-gold curls glowed darkly on his neck, and his head was covered in 100 crimson threads matted with gems. He had four dimples in each cheek – yellow, green, crimson and blue. He also had seven bright pupils – eye jewels in each kingly eye. Each foot had seven toes and each hand seven fingers. His nails had the grip of a hawk's claw.

He wore a fitted purple mantle, folded three times and held at his breast by a brooch of light-gold and silver, adorned with gold inlays. It was a source of light for the warriors to look at. A silk tunic covered him down to his apron of dark-red silk. He sported a deep-crimson shield (five discs within a light-gold rim) and a sword hung on his belt, its ivory guard decorated with gold.

Near him in the chariot was a fierce javelin, grey-bladed with a hard point, riveted with bright gold. He held in one hand nine human heads and in the other hand ten. He shook them to show the result of one night's warfare against the four provinces of Erin.

The women of Connaught and Munster climbed on their own men in order to see Cúchulainn, but Maeve did not see him. She did not dare to show her face from under the barrel-shaped shelter of shields, for she was afraid of him. She could not see the boy that they were making so much of. She asked Fergus what kind of man he was.

A chant started, and Maeve climbed up on the men's backs to see him.

Dubthach said at this time, "Is this the Warped One? We will have corpses and shrieks in our enclosures and tales to tell. There will be stones over their graves and dead kings increasing. You might fight this Brave One but you are now lost. I see his wild shape and his heap of spoils, nine heads in one hand, and ten more – his treasure. Your women climb up and reveal their faces, but great Queen Maeve shuns the bitter battle. If I had my way all the armies would put an end to the Warped One."

Fergus exclaimed, "Get Dubthach with his black tongue behind the army. Since the maiden massacre he has done only harm. It was terrible slaughter when he killed Conchobor's son Fiacha, and no better when he slew Coirpre mac Feidlimid. Now this son of Lugaid lags in the battle against Ulster. Those that he could not kill he sets at one another's throats. All the exiles will cry out, the laughter of their beardless son, but soon the host of Ulster will come and harass them like herds of cattle – his councils scattered far and wide by risen Ulster in its pangs. There will be stories of great slaughter and the moaning of great queens. There will be mangling of wounds and mounds made of the slain. There will be corpses all around and the ravens will have their meat. There will be shields scattered on the slopes and great sorrowing. The blood of men will be poured out over the ground. They will wander far indeed in exile from Ulster, their home."

Fergus flung Dubthach from him, and he fell silent near a group of soldiers.

Ailill asked him why he was so fierce because of Ulster cows and women. He could sense great slaughter and butchery, though it was one by one they died in the ford that day.

Maeve replied, "Rise up, Ailill, and guard your cattle. The grinning boy was storming in turmoil by the brinks of fords, with wide graves and dark pools. Valorous Fergus and Ulster's exiles will have their due when the battle is over."

Fergus said not to pay heed to stupid women. They would be buried and their deaths would cool his fever and he should fight fair.

The poet Gabrán said, "Why make a show of words for queen and followers? They will have a taste of battle, but there is one you must pin down or he will earn hatred."

"Do not flinch from him," Fergus said. "Go and meet him at the ford."

Maeve said, "Wait until we hear from Ailill."

Ailill said that Fergus knew this land, and he brings shame on their heads; he would not lead their cattle round but hacked and plundered round them and swore that he did not take them by many long ways.

Fergus said that after a year the noble Maeve should not be blamed.

Fiacha Fialdána ('the bold and true') went to speak with his cousin Maine Andoe. Dóchae mac Mágach arrived with Maine Andoe and Dubthach from Ulster. Dóchae threw a javelin at Fiacha, but it hit his friend Dubthach. Fiacha threw a javelin at Dóchae, but it hit his kinsman instead. The place where this happened has been called Imroll Belag Eóin. Some believe that Imroll Belach Eóin got its name later when the men of Ulster had recovered from their pangs.

The two armies had arrived and settled at Belach Eóin when Dairmait, Conchobor's son, came out from the north. He said to send out a horseman.

"If Maine comes," he said, "I will meet him and we can parley."

They met, and Dairmait said he had come from Conchobor to tell Maeve and Ailill to set the cattle free and make restitution.

"Let them bring their bull here in the east and have them to fight, as Maeve promised," he said.

Maine said he would go and tell them.

Dairmait challenged Maine and each of them threw his javelin at the other. Both of them died. Some say this is how Belach Eóin got its name.

The armies rushed against each other and sixty warriors were killed. The name Ard in Dírma means 'the armies' height'.

Aengus, son of Aenlám Gaibe, a brave Ulster warrior, turned the entire army aside at Muid Loga, which is called Lugmod today. Ath Da Ferta means 'the ford of the two grave mounds'. Aengus refused to let them pass. He pelted them with flagstones. Some say that if they agreed to hand-to-hand combat, the whole army would have perished at his hands before they could come to Emain Macha. However, there were no rules of fair play for him, and he was overwhelmed.

Cúchulainn cried out to send someone out to him.

They all cried, "Not I! Not I! Why should I be the one?"

Fergus mac Róich was asked to fight him, but he did not want to fight his foster-son, Cúchulainn. Wine was served and he became drunk, and he was asked again to proceed into combat. This time he went, because they had begged him.

Cúchulainn pointed out that Fergus had no sword in his scabbard, and Fergus replied that it made no difference. If he had a sword in it, he would not use it on Cúchulainn.

Cúchulainn retreated from Fergus as far as a swamp on condition that Fergus would give way to him on the day of the impending battle. Cúchulainn ran off into the swamp, which was called Grellac Dollaid.

"Chase him!" Fergus was urged, but Fergus said that he would not, for it was not easy. He said he would proceed after him when his turn came round again.

Now they all went past Cúchulainn encamped at Crích Rois.

Ferchu Loingsech was a Connaught man who was always

troubling Maeve and Ailill. From the day Ailill assumed the kingship he had not once visited their camp, even when he was in dire straits. He was always pillaging their borderlands when they were absent.

It happened that he was east of Ai with his troop of about a dozen men. He heard that the armies of the four provinces of Erin had been stopped and held from the Monday at the end of summer to the beginning of spring by one man, who killed a man at the ford each day and 100 men each night.

Ferchu and his warriors went to find Cúchulainn, and when they found him they fought foul. All 12 fell on him together. Cúchulainn fought back and struck off their 12 heads. He planted stones for them in the ground, setting a head on each stone. There was a stone for Ferchu Loingsech's head as well.

Next day Maeve sent twenty-nine men against Cúchulainn in the swamp of Fuiliarnn, near Ferdia's ford. The men were Gaile Dána, his twenty-seven sons, and his sister's son, Glas mac Delga. They said that it should be counted as single combat since the sons of Gaile Dána were all one, limb and limb, flesh and flesh.

Fergus uttered a long sigh. He told his warriors that he thought Cúchulainn would be killed.

"But", they cried out, "who will kill him?"

"Gaile Dána", he said, "and his twenty-seven sons and his sister's son, Glas mac Delga. Every one of the warriors has put poison on all his weapons. Any man they wound will die in nine days at most, if he does not die at once. If anyone brings me news of Cúchulainn's death, he can have my weapons with my blessing."

Fiacha mac Fir-Febe said he would go.

Gaile Dána rose up early in the morning with his twenty-seven sons and his sister's son, Glas mac Delga. They went to seek out Cúchulainn. Fiacha mac Fir-Febe went out also.

Gaile Dána found Cúchulainn and they flung all their twenty-nine spears at him. All the spears were on target, but Cúchulainn performed the rim-feat with his shield and all the spears fell without harming him.

Cúchulainn pulled his sword from his scabbard to cut away the spears from his shield and lighten the load, and while he was doing this they attacked him with their fists. They struck him down and his face met the ford's sandy gravel. He screamed out a warrior's cry, so that everyone in Ulster should hear it, except those that were asleep.

Fiacha leaped from his chariot when he saw their hands raised against Cúchulainn, and he cut off the hands of all twenty-nine. He was in the nick of time.

Cúchulainn swore by the gods that not one of the twenty-nine would get back to camp alive while he drew breath. Cúchulainn, with the two sons of Ficce, killed all twenty-nine.

So ended the battle with Cúchulainn on the Táin. On a stone in the middle of the ford there is a mark caused by Cúchulainn shield and the marks of their fists and knees. Twenty-nine standing stones were erected at that place for the dead men.

Chapter 16

Ferdia Versus Cúchulainn

The leaders of the four provinces of Erin argued about who should go against Cúchulainn at the ford. They all agreed that it should be the horn-skinned warrior from Irrus Domnann. There was not a feat of Cúchulainn's that he lacked, except the *gae bolga*. They thought this might have saved his life for no weapon could pierce it.

Maeve sent messengers to Ferdia, but he would not come back with them. Therefore she sent poets and bards to bring the blushes to his cheeks with mockery and insult, so there would be nowhere for him to lay his head in peace. Eventually he came back with them to Maeve and Ailill's tent, which had been pitched on the Táin.

Their daughter Finnabair was sat beside him, and she handed him drinks with three kisses for every cup. She offered him fragrant apples, saying that he was her darling and her chosen one above all the world.

When Ferdia was full of good humour, Maeve said, "Well now, Ferdia, do you know why you have been brought to the tent?"

Ferdia said, "The noblest men in Ulster are here, so why should I not be here too?"

Maeve tempted him with a chariot worth twenty-seven bondmaids, war-harnesses for a dozen men, and a portion of the plain of Ai equal to the plain of Murtheimne. He would be able to stay for ever in Cruachan, with wine supplied, and he and his relations would be free from taxation. She showed him her leaf-shaped brooch, which was made out of ten score ounces of gold. All these things would be his, and Finnabair would be his wife, if he defeated Cúchulainn.

Ferdia replied that he would sooner leave these riches with her than go out and fight his own foster-brother. Maeve knew well how to stir up strife. She told Ferdia that Cúchulainn had boasted that he would not count it any great victory to defeat Ferdia.

"He should not have said that," Ferdia said. "By the gods, I shall be at the ford tomorrow to fight him."

Maeve was very pleased that the promise had been made.

She started to sing: riches and rings she promised them, a share of woods and plains, privilege for their kinsfolk to the end of the age. Did it take their breath away, Ferdia mac Damán? It was theirs. They should accept it, for others had.

Ferdia replied that he was no hollow hero. "Tomorrow I shall go to bear a terrible trial," he said.

Maeve said she knew he would kill Cúchulainn when he met him.

Ferdia cried out that he would pick six heroes before he tried his strength in front of the armies. If she would grant this, he said, he would fight the Hound of Ulster.

Maeve said he could take farmers and soldiers, or Niaman to the slaughter or choose from among the bards. If he wished, he could have Morann or Coirpre nia Manann or his own two sons.

Ferdia remarked that there was no doubt he would be master on the mounds of Cruachan! By his strength he would take the speckled silk, the gold and silver and everything he had been promised.

Maeve said he was the choicest of champions, and she offered him a round brooch. She told him he should rest until the following Sunday, when the fight was due. He was her fiercest and finest warrior, and all should be given into his hands, including the world's greatest jewels and queenly Finnabair, the hero's favourite.

"When the Hound is exhausted, everything will be mine," said Ferdia.

Fergus mac Róich was there while they were bargaining.

He went to his tent and said, "A sad deed will be done tomorrow morning. His own beloved foster-brother mac Damán is preparing to fight him. Would one of you, in pity for Cúchulainn, go to him with my blessing and warn him to flee from the ford tomorrow morning?"

Everyone he asked said they would not go on such an errand, even if Fergus himself had been due to fight at the ford. Fergus therefore went himself to warm Cúchulainn.

When Cúchulainn heard the news he said he wished to avoid the fight – not because he feared Ferdia, but because he loved him so much. Fergus said he would do well to fear Ferdia too, for he had a skin of horn that no point of the sword could pierce.

"You need not worry," Cúchulainn said. "If he appears at the ford, his joints and limbs will bend like reeds in the river at the point of my sword."

So they spoke together and sang. Fergus said it was time they were astir. Ferdia mac Damáine was coming, and his face was red with rage against Cúchulainn.

Cúchulainn sang out that he had stood his ground there through many single combats.

Fergus warned Cúchulainn again that Ferdia wore a skin that no weapon could pierce, but Cúchulainn said he would fight nevertheless.

Fergus said that Ferdia's brave arm was strong with rage, and he held a blood-covered sword. He was as strong as 100 men.

Cúchulainn cried out to Fergus, "Say no more! There are no odds too great for me in any part of Ireland. I am not one for boasting, but I swear now that I shall be victorious over Damán mac Dáire's son."

Fergus said that he had turned against Ulster to avenge a wrong. Heroes and warriors had left their homes to come with him.

Cúchulainn answered that if it hadn't been for Conchobor's

pangs Maeve's journey from Scáil Plain would have been even more of a trail of tears.

When Fergus had gone, Laeg asked Cúchulainn what he would do, and Cúchulainn said that when Ferdia came to attack him he would be washed and bathed, with hair nicely plaited and freshly trimmed, as the armies of the four provinces of Erin would all be there to watch the fight.

Sweet-haired Emer was waiting in the Meadow of the Oxen, at Sliab Fuait, so he spent the night with her.

As far as Ferdia was concerned, he went to his tent and told his followers of the pledge he had given Maeve. He was committed to single combat with Cúchulainn the next day, and six warriors would go with him to make sure he carried out his promise.

The people in Ferdia's tent that night were depressed. They were certain that if these two contenders met, there would be a double downfall. It was no easy task fighting Cúchulainn on the Táin.

Great anxieties weighed upon Ferdia that night, so he could not get to sleep. He was afraid he might lose the treasure and the girl in combat with this one man; if he did not fight Cúchulainn, he would have to fight the six warriors. However, he had a greater worry that his life and his head would never be in his own hands if he appeared at the ford before Cúchulainn.

Ferdia woke early next day and said to his charioteer to bring the horses and yoke the chariot. The charioteer swore that he would be better off not making this journey. Ferdia talked with his charioteer and encouraged him. They started to chant.

Ferdia said he would meet with Cúchulainn, and he would pierce his slight body and the spear would pass through him so that he would die.

The charioteer said that these were fierce threats, but it would be better to stay where they were or they would die. He would go to disaster before all of Ulster and the feat would be long remembered.

Ferdia said he wasted his breath. It was a warrior's duty not to be shy or meek. He would not hold back.

"Silence, my friend. Have courage to the end," he said. "Let us start the battle."

The charioteer got his horses and yoked the chariot and they left camp.

Ferdia said, "Wait a moment. It is not right to go without saying farewell to the men of Erin. Turn the horses and chariot round to face them."

The charioteer did so three times and he faced the men of Erin.

Maeve asked Ailill if he heard his son-in-law bidding him farewell.

"Is that what he was doing?" Ailill said.

Maeve replied that it was. She swore by the vow of her people that the man making his farewell there would not be coming back on his own feet.

"We did well with the marriage agreement," Ailill said. "If he kills Cúchulainn, it is all the same to us if they both die."

Ferdia proceeded to the ford.

"See if Cúchulainn is at the ford," Ferdia said, but the charioteer said he was not there. "Look well," Ferdia said.

"Cúchulainn is not such a little speck that one cannot see him if he is out there," the charioteer said.

"True enough!" said Ferdia, "but Cúchulainn never had a real warrior against him on the Táin Bó Cúailnge until this day. As soon as he heard us coming he must have left the ford."

"It is a shame to slander Cúchulainn in his absence," the charioteer said. "Don't you remember when he was fighting the harsh Germán Garbglas above the border of the Tyrrhene Sea? He left his sword with the enemy forces, then he killed 100 warriors to reach it and bring it back. At Scáthach's house the steward gave him a blow with his three-pronged flesh-fork in the small of his back and sent him flying out like a stone past the door. Cúchulainn went back in and hit the brute a blow with his sword, cutting him in two."

Ferdia said, "You have done wrong not to have reminded him of this. He would not come looking for a fight. Pull the shafts of the chariot alongside now, and place the skin covering under my head so that I can sleep."

The charioteer said, "Alas for your rest! You would sleep as well in the path of a stag hunt!"

"Why, boy, can you not keep watch for me?"

The charioteer said that he could, and he would give Ferdia warning of Cúchulainn's arrival, unless he came out of the clouds.

The chariot shafts were pulled along by his side, and the skin covering was placed under his head, but he could not sleep, not even a wink.

Meanwhile Cúchulainn asked Laeg to bring the horses and yoke the chariot. "If Ferdia is waiting, he will be wondering what has kept us," Cúchulainn said.

The charioteer brought the horses and the chariot. Cúchulainn mounted it and they pressed on towards the ford.

Ferdia's charioteer had not been watching long before he heard the creaking of the chariot as it drew near.

He awoke Ferdia and started to chant: "I hear that a chariot is creaking; I see its yoke of silver and the great body of a man above the hard prow. The shafts jut forward and they are approaching us by the place of the tree stump, they seem triumphant and proud. There is a skilled Hound at the helm, a fine chariot-warrior, a wild hawk hurrying his horses southward. Surely it is Cúchulainn's chariot coming. Who said he was not coming to his defeat? He had a dream the year before: whoever, at the appointed time, opposes the Hound on the slope, let him be cautious. The Hound of Emain Macha, in all his different shapes, the Hound of plunder and battle."

Ferdia told his charioteer that he praised Cúchulainn too much.

He said, "Get my weapons ready to meet him at the ford."

Ferdia chanted further: "It is your help I need now, not this false friendship. Enough of his praises! We're all the same if we are dead. Let Cúailnge's great warrior come in his glory, and we shall dispose of him."

The charioteer said, "Cúailnge's great warrior travels in his glory toward us. Give praise where it is due."

Ferdia said, "There will be blows between us. You have not stopped praising Cúchulainn since we set out."

They met in the middle of the ford not long after that, and Ferdia said to Cúchulainn, "You are welcome."

Cúchulainn said, "I could trust your welcome once, but I do not trust it now. It was not for you, Ferdia, to bid me welcome. This is my homeland, and you are the intruder. You are wrong to challenge me to combat. You have driven out the women and young men and boys as well as their troops of horses, their herds and their flocks and all their goods."

Ferdia said, "That is enough! What brought you to meet me in this warlike combat? When you were with Scáthach, Uathach and Aife you were only my servant. You fixed my spears and made my bed."

Cúchulainn said, "This is true, but I did it because I was young and small. You cannot call me that now. There is no warrior in existence I am not able to face."

They reproached each other and curtailed their friendship, and Ferdia chanted with Cúchulainn answering.

"What brings you here, to test my strength? You will regret that you came. You are a fire without fuel, and you will need plenty of help if you ever see home."

Cúchulainn answered, "Like a great boar before a herd I shall overwhelm you before the armies. I shall punish you and bring havoc upon your head."

Ferdia said, "I shall kill you. I shall destroy you and drive you to flight before all eyes."

Cúchulainn answered, "Must we start our fight by groaning over corpses? Come what may, let us enter the ford to face death before the armies with bloody spears."

Ferdia said, "Before nightfall I shall fight you at Bairche. The men of Ulster will cry out when death seizes you. The fearful sight will pierce them."

Cúchulainn exclaimed, "You have reached your doom! Your hour has come. My sword shall slash, and you will fall at a hero's hands. Never again will you lead men."

Ferdia said, "Little boy, you have boasted and threatened enough. You will find no mercy or victory here. I know you to be a chicken-hearted young boy."

Cúchulainn said, "When we were with Scáthach we proceeded as one with a common outlook. You were my bosom friend and I shall miss you."

Ferdia said, "Make much of yourself, but the fight is to come. Cúchulainn of Cúailnge has lost his common sense and he will suffer for it. The guilt will be his."

Cúchulainn said, "You do wrong to try to fight me. This is only Ailill and Maeve's ill-doing. It has gone badly with all those who have come against me – I have killed them all. Ferdia, son of Damán, fierce warrior, do not fight, for you will suffer more than I shall, and you will bring sorrow to your people. Here you will find your resting place. How can it be possible that you alone will escape my temper. I shall overcome you, despite your mighty deeds and your rage. Son of Damán, you will never have the girl you were boasting about – Maeve's daughter Finnabair. All her fairness of body will never yield to your assault. Finnabair, the royal daughter, is nothing but a snare. She played false with others and ruined them as she will ruin you. Do not break our friendship and our bond. Do not break the oath that has been made. Noble warrior, do not fight. The same girl was promised falsely to fifty men. They got nothing but my spear as I showed them to their graves. Ferbaeth, they said, was brave enough and had a house full of fine heroes, but a short moment quenched his fire. I finished him with one blow. Srúbdaire found a bitter end, and 100 women held him dear. There was a time when his fame was high, but he would not be saved. This is the reason you should not come to fight me, Ferdia.

When we were with Scáthach, Uathach and Aife, we always went out together to do battle, to go into the forests and deserts, dark with mysteries. We made our bed and slept one sleep in the foreign lands after battle. In those days you were not concerned with cunning, but if our friendship is to be finished through foul play, you should prepare to face your first defeat.

We should forget we are foster-brothers."

Ferdia said, "We have talked too much. What weapons shall we use today?"

Cúchulainn said, "You have the choice of weapons because you reached the ford first."

"Do you recall", Ferdia said, "the last feat we learned while with Scáthach, Uathach and Aife?"

Cúchulainn said, "I remember it well. Let us set to."

They took up their two finely marked feat-playing shields and their eight shields with the sharp rims, their eight darts, their ivory-hilted swords and their eight small ivory darts. They were busy with these feats from early morning to midday, attacking each other, but bringing each other's efforts to nothing with the knobs and bosses of their feat-shields.

Ferdia said to Cúchulainn, "We should change the rules. We shall settle nothing by this means of combat."

They threw their shields, darts and swords to their charioteers, and Ferdia asked what weapons they should use next.

Cúchulainn said, "You still have the choice of weapons until nightfall, since you were first at the ford."

Ferdia said, "Let us try the smooth-polished spears, bound with tight flax."

They took up their shields and hurled spears at one another from midday until sunset. They wounded each other but neither of them would yield.

Then Ferdia said to Cúchulainn, "It is time to break off."

They broke off and flung their weapons into the chariots. Then they came up to each other and put their arms around each other's necks and gave three kisses. Their horses were stabled there for the whole night and the charioteers used the same fire. Their charioteers made up fresh beds of rushes for them, with rests for their heads, suitable for wounded men. Doctors came to attend to them and dropped wholesome healing herbs into their wounds. Cúchulainn had countless wounds, but he sent the doctors to Ferdia on the west side of the ford. If he won, he didn't want it to be because he had received more care. Ferdia, out of all the health-giving food and delicious drinks that the men of Erin gave him, sent an equal share over to Cúchulainn on the north side of the ford. Ferdia had a better supply of food than Cúchulainn. The men of Erin were supplying Ferdia because they wanted to protect him from Cúchulainn. Only the people of Breg Plain were supplying Cúchulainn.

The two warriors rose early next morning and went down to the battle ford. Cúchulainn asked Ferdia what weapons they would use today, and Ferdia said it was Cúchulainn's turn to have the choice of weapons until nightfall.

Cúchulainn said, "Let us try our large stabbing spears. Let our horses be brought and our chariots made ready."

"Let us begin," said Ferdia.

With their two solid shields and their heavy stabbing spears they fought each other from early morning until sunset.

By the time the sun set, the charioteers were dazed and the great heroes themselves needed a rest. Ferdia said that it was time to have a break, and eventually Cúchulainn agreed.

"Why should we struggle like Fomorian giants? Let the turmoil die away," he said.

Ferdia said, "Very well, let us break off."

Once again they broke off and they threw their weapons into their charioteers' arms. They put their arms around each other's necks and gave three kisses. The horses stayed the night in the same paddock and their charioteers by the same fire. Doctors came to attend to their injuries. So extensive were their wounds that the only thing to be done was to lay magic amulets on them and recite spells to stop the spurts of blood. For each amulet, spell or charm that was laid upon Cúchulainn's wounds he had the same sent to Ferdia on the west side of the ford. The men of Erin gave Ferdia food and mouth-watering drinks, and the same was sent over to Cúchulainn on the north side of the ford.

They rose early the next morning and arrived at the ford for battle. Cúchulainn saw evil and darkness over Ferdia. Ferdia said that Cúchulainn had a dreadful look. A shadow had fallen on his hair overnight and his eyes had grown dull. All his fine shape and strength had gone.

Ferdia said his appearance wasn't caused by any dread of Cúchulainn. There was not a warrior in Ireland that he could not defeat.

Cúchulainn lamented, and he started to chant with Ferdia.

He said, "I knew it was your doom when a woman sent you here to fight against your foster-brother."

Ferdia replied, "Cúchulainn, you are wise and a true hero – a great warrior. Everyone must at last come to the sod that is to be his last bed."

Cúchulainn said, "Maeve's daughter Finnabair – whatever beauty she might possess – was never promised to you for love."

Ferdia said, "My strength has been well used by now. Never until this day have I found such a hero."

Cúchulainn cried out, "You are to blame for what might come about. You are the son of Damán mac Dáire, coming at a woman's word to cross swords with your foster-brother. There is no woman that ever ate, no man that was ever born, no son of a king or queen for whose sake I will do harm."

Ferdia said, "Cúchulainn, son of bravery, I shall win renown and no one will think I am at fault."

Cúchulainn concluded that his heart was a knot of blood, and his soul was tearing at his body.

"I would rather face 1,000 fights, Ferdia, than this fight with you."

"You may blame me all you like today," said Ferdia. "What weapons shall we use?"

Cúchulainn replied that Ferdia had the choice of weapons until nightfall.

"Then", Ferdia said, "let us take up our massive stroke-dealing swords, so that the end might come this day. Hacking strokes might serve us better than yesterday's stabbing."

Cúchulainn said, "Let us begin."

They took up their two great stroke-dealing swords and began hacking, striking and destroying. They cut pieces from their shoulders.

They fought with each other in this way from early morning until sunset.

Then Ferdia said to Cúchulainn, "Let us break off from this." Cúchulainn said, "Very well."

They broke off and flung their spears into their chariots. That morning they had been two solid men, lively and serene; they parted that night woeful and weary – two wasted men.

The horses passed the night in different paddocks and the charioteers did not pass the night at the same fire.

Ferdia arose early next morning and came out alone to the ford. He knew that this day would decide the fight. Or both of them would die. He put on his battle-harness before Cúchulainn came out to meet him. He wore a flimsy girdle of silk with a dark supple apron of leather over his tunic. For fear of the *gae bolga* he also put on a sturdy apron of iron. He placed upon his head his crested battle-helmet, well decorated with forty precious carbuncles and inlaid with red enamel and precious stones from the East. He took up in his left hand his great spear, stout and fierce. In his right hand he took his battle-sword with its hilt of red-gold. On his back he carried his huge shield with the great red-gold knob in the middle and another fifty knobs around it, each big enough to hide a prize boar.

That day Ferdia performed 1,000 different feats that no one had ever taught him – not his foster-mother nor his foster-father, nor Scáthach, nor Uathach, nor Aife.

Cúchulainn came to the ford and observed Ferdia's 1,000 thrilling feats, which were entirely miraculous.

Cúchulainn said to Laeg, "Look at the 1,000 feats that Ferdia performs. He is going to use them today on me."

Now Cúchulainn too put on his battle-gear and he too did 1,000 thrilling feats that he had learned from no one. Ferdia saw the feats and knew they were all for him.

"What weapons shall we use, Ferdia?" Cúchulainn asked.

Ferdia said that Cúchulainn had the choice of weapons until

nightfall. Cúchulainn said they should fight together in the ford, and Ferdia agreed. Ferdia, though he spoke softly, knew this was the worst thing for him, for Cúchulainn had destroyed many warriors in the waters.

Great things were done by the two heroes that day in the ford. Those two great warriors of the west were like two blazing torches of bravery in Ireland. They were the cream of Ireland's valour flung together from afar by the ill-doing of Ailill and Maeve.

They started to work feats on one another. From the grey and dewy dawn until noon the warriors' madness mounted.

Cúchulainn sprang straight from the brink of the ford on to the shield knob of Ferdia mac Damán so that he could strike the edge of his shield at Ferdia's head. Ferdia struck Cúchulainn and sent him flying from him like a bird. Another blow sent Cúchulainn sprawling like a little boy into the ford.

Laeg called out, "Your enemy shook you as easily as a loving mother slaps her son! He tossed you aside as if he was cleaning a cup in a tub! He crushed you like a mill crushing fine malt. He pounced on you like a hawk on a little bird!"

Cúchulainn rose up, swift as the wind, swift as a swallow in a storm. He landed on the knob of Ferdia's shield and tried to strike him down over his shield-rim. Ferdia gave a shake of his shield and Cúchulainn was tossed into the middle of the ford. Cúchulainn was in a fury. He swelled like a bladder full of breath. He bent himself in a hideous arch, mottled and terrifying, and the huge hero loomed up over Ferdia, vast as a Fomorian giant.

They fought together so closely that their heads and feet touched. Their shields split, their spears bent, and their shield-rims and sword hilts and spear-shafts screamed like demons. So closely did they fight that they drove the river off its course and out of its bed, leaving a dirt space in the middle of the ford large enough for the burial place of a king or queen. There was not a drop of water in it except what the two heroes splashed there in their fighting in the ford. So closely did they fight that the horses of the men of Erin broke loose in panic. They broke their shackle-hoops, hobbles, reins and ropes, and the women and children, the ill and the imbeciles, broke out south-westward from the camp of the men of Erin.

While they were busy with the sharp sword edges, Ferdia saw a chance to kill Cúchulainn. He dealt him a blow with his ivory-hilted straight sword, and buried it in Cúchulainn's breast. Blood ran over his belt and the ford went crimson with the warrior's gore. All of Ferdia's strokes had worn him out. He called out to Laeg mac Riangabra for the *gae bolga*.

When Ferdia heard Cúchulainn calling for the *gae bolga*, he dropped his shield to cover the lower part of his body. Cúchulainn took his short javelin and hurled it over the rim of Ferdia's shield and the edge of his horn skin, driving it in such a manner that it pierced Ferdia's heart.

Ferdia raised his shield up, but it was too late.

The charioteer sent the *gae bolga* down the stream.

He said, "Beware of the *gae bolga*."

Cúchulainn caught it in the fork of his foot and sent it towards Ferdia. It went through the sturdy apron of twice-smelted iron, and it shattered into three parts a large stone, the size of a millstone. It passed through the highways and byways of Ferdia's body.

Ferdia said that this was enough, for now he would die. He said that there was strength in Cúchulainn's right foot.

He chanted: "Hound of the bright deeds, you have killed me unfairly."

His ribs were broken, and his heart was all blood.

Cúchulainn ran to Ferdia and clasped his arms around him, and there by Ferdia's head he fainted away into a trance.

Laeg saw this and he saw how all the men of Erin rose up.

"Get up now, Cúchulainn," said Laeg, "for the men of Erin are coming to attack."

But they were not thinking of a fight at that moment. Now that he had killed Ferdia mac Damán mac Dáire, he saw no reason to rise.

The men of Erin chanted: "Rise up, slaughter-hound of Emain Macha. You must recover. Have more spirit. You have felled Ferdia in a great combat."

Cúchulainn answered, "What have I to do with spirit? Sorrow

is weighing me down after the deed that I have done, for I have hacked Ferdia harshly."

Laeg said, "You have nothing to regret; indeed, you ought to boast about it."

Cúchulainn said, "Alas, Ferdia will never draw another breath!"

Laeg answered, "The women of the Craebruad would not have it otherwise. Ferdia is dead and you are alive."

Cúchulainn said, "From the first day I left Cúailnge to come against Maeve she has had carnage and renown with all the warriors that have been slain."

Laeg concluded, "You have had no sound sleep since you stopped at the great Táin. There were so few to help, and you woke many warriors early in the morning."

Cúchulainn began to mourn for Ferdia. He said, "Alas! Woe to you! Before we fought together he did not listen to anyone who knew my great deeds. Woe to you, Laeg mac Riangabra! You did not chide him with thoughts of our fighting together. Woe to him that ignored Fergus's well-meant warning! Woe to him that proud King Conall, much skilled in arms, did not help with words of their fostering together! Those were men that would not run to him with news of false promises from any fair-headed Connaught woman. Those were men who knew that none of human birth, until doomsday, could ever match the great deeds that he did with his shield or shield-rim, sword or dart, draughts or chess, horse or chariot. Never would the hand of a warrior hack the flesh from a hero like the honoured heir Ferdia. However, would the red-mouthed Badb cry out like this at the day of doom in the gap of battle? Never until doomsday would anyone fighting for Cruachan get the bargain he had obtained for defending it."

Cúchulainn arose from beside Ferdia's head and said, "Well, Ferdia, that was a great day of doom. The men of Erin sent you against me, but it is no easy thing to struggle and strive with Cúchulainn on the Táin Bó Cúailnge. Ferdia is dead as a result of our fight, but life has to go on. I must live to mourn his everlasting loss. When we were with Scáthach in Scotland, learning feats, it seemed as if our friendship would remain unbroken until the day of doom. I loved the noble way he blushed and I loved his perfect form. I loved his blue eyes, his way of speech and his skill in combat. His like never moved to the tearing fray and was never seized with wrath, nor bore shield upon his back. Never until this day, Ferdia, did I ever find your match for great deeds in combat. Maeve's daughter Finnabair, whatever beauty she possesses, was an empty offering, Ferdia."

Cúchulainn stayed there staring at Ferdia.

At last Cúchulainn said, "Well, friend Laeg, strip Ferdia now. Take off his garments. Let me see the brooch fought for in this battle."

Laeg stripped Ferdia and took off his gear and garments, showing Cúchulainn the brooch. Cúchulainn lamented, saying to Ferdia that the hosts mourned his conquering arm and their fostering together. He was a sight to please a prince with his gold-rimmed shield and slender sword. There was a ring of bright silver on his fine hand and he had skill in chess and his cheeks were flushed. His curled yellow hair was like a lovely jewel, and he wore a leaf-shaped belt at his waist. The shield did not save him that he brought to the fight. Their struggle was shameful, with grief and uproar.

Cúchulainn now said, "Friend Laeg, cut Ferdia open and take the *gae bolga* out of him, for I need my weapon."

Laeg proceeded to cut Ferdia open, and he took out the *gae bolga*.

Cúchulainn saw his weapon crimson and bloody from Ferdia's body, and he chanted: "Ill met, Ferdia, your blood in my sight and me with my weapon unwiped."

When they were beyond the sea, Scáthach's and Uathach's pupils witnessed a struggle between them. Cúchulainn recalled how Scáthach cried out to proceed to the field of battle.

Then he said to Ferdia and to Lugaid of the lavish hand and to fond, foolish Ferbaeth, "Let him go and meet Germán."

At the battle rock on the slope above the Lake of Envy they took 400 men from the islands of Victory. He stood with Ferdia in the door of Germán's fort and slew a number of warriors. Ferbaeth killed Bláth mac Colbair of the red sword on the slope. Grim, swift

Lugaid slew Mugairne from the Tyrrhene coast.

The chanting continued: "They went in and killed 200 men. Ferdia killed Dam Dreimend and Dam Dílenn, who were cruel. They destroyed Germán's cunning fort above the wide, glittering sea and they took Germán alive to Scáthach of the great shield.

In fair Elga their famous foster-mother bound them in a blood pact of friendship, so that rage would never come between them. Sad and pitiful was the day that saw Ferdia's strength spent and brought the downfall of a friend. He poured him some red blood! If Cúchulainn had met his death fighting with Greek warriors, he would not have outlasted him; he would have died at his side. Misery had befallen them – two foster-sons of Scáthach. Cúchulainn was broken and blood-red. Ferdia's chariot stood empty. Misery had befallen the two foster-sons of Scáthach. Ferdia was dead and Cúchulainn was alive. Braver was battle-madness!

Laeg said, "Well, let us leave the ford now, for we have been too long at this place."

"Very well, let us leave it," Cúchulainn said.

All the other struggles and contests that he ever fought seemed only playful games after his struggle with Ferdia.

He said these words: "It was all play, all sport, until Ferdia arrived at the ford."

A like leaning they both had, similar rights, the same belongings, the same well-intentioned foster-mother, whose name was much honoured. They had the same force and fury and the same feats of war. Scáthach had awarded two shields, one to Cúchulainn and one to Ferdia.

Cúchulainn cried out, "Misery!"

A pillar of gold he had levelled in the ford in tribute to Ferdia, the bull of the tribe-herd, braver than any other warrior, fiery and dangerous as a lion.

"Yesterday he was a mountain slope; today he is only a shadow," Cúchulainn said.

He had killed countless multitudes, choice cattle, choice men, choice horses. The great force that came from warlike Cruachan had lost between a half and a third of its warriors.

Chapter 17

Ulster Reacts

The horses went off southward from Ferdia's ford, and Cúchulainn lay there sick. Senoll Uathach ('the hideous') and the two sons of Ficce were the first to reach him. They carried him back to Conaille, where they nursed his wounds and bathed them in the refreshing waters of the River Sas.

While Cúchulainn was washing in the waters, the armies pitched camp at Imorach Smiromrach ('the mass of marrow'). Mac Roth left the armies and travelled northward to keep watch over the men of Ulster. He went as far as Sliab Fuait to see if anyone was following. He came back with the news that there was only one chariot. Mac Roth said he had seen a chariot crossing the plain from the north, and the man in the chariot had silvery-grey hair and sported no weapon but a silver spike in one hand. He drove a brightly coloured chariot. In front of him ran a hunting dog.

Ailill asked Fergus, "Do you think it is Conchobor or Celtchar?"

Fergus said, "No, I think it is Cethern, Fintan's son, a man of great violence and a bloody blade."

Fergus was right. Cethern hurled himself directly at the camp and killed many warriors. He himself was wounded badly, and he came back from the battle with his guts around his feet.

A fresh bed of roses was fixed for him, with a pillow, and Cúchulainn sent Laeg to the enemy camp to ask Fiacha mac Fir-

Febe for a doctor. He said he would kill them all if they refused, no matter where they hid themselves.

The doctors went across one at a time to visit him, but Cethern struck them with his fists. He slew fifty healers in this way (some say it was fifteen), but the last of them received a glancing blow and fell stunned. Cúchulainn had saved his life.

Cethern said he killed the doctors because they gave him bad news. The great healer Fingin, Conchobor's own doctor, came to examine Cúchulainn and Cethern. Cúchulainn warned him to watch out for Cethern, for he had killed fifty other healers. Fingin observed Cethern from a distance.

"What made the wound?" Fingin asked.

"A vain, arrogant woman," Cethern replied. "She was a tall, long-faced woman with pretty features and long yellow hair. She had two gold birds on her shoulders, and she wore a purple cloak folded about her, with gold on her back. She sported a light, stinging lance in her hand, and she held an iron sword with a woman's grip over her head. She was massive."

Cúchulainn said he recognised the description. It was Maeve of Cruachan.

Cethern also had another wound, but it was not serious.

He said that it had been caused by a warrior with a curved shield in his hand and an iron-bladed sword. He wore a brown cloak wrapped around him, held with a silver brooch.

Cúchulainn said that sounded like Illann, Fergus mac Róich's son.

Cethern said that another wound was the work of two men. They had come at him together. They carried long shields. They also had tough silver chains and a silver belt each, and five-pronged spears. Each had a collar of silver.

Cúchulainn said, "I am sure they must be Oll and Oichne, two of Ailill and Maeve's foster-sons. Every time they go into battle someone falls by their hands.

Cethern said, "Two more warriors will fall by their hands, bright and noble and manly in looks."

Cúchulainn said, "I know them. They are amongst the King's most trusted servants."

Fingin said, "The blood is black here. They have speared Cethern through his heart at an angle and made a cross inside him. I cannot promise to cure this, but there are a couple of possible remedies." Fingin asked, "Was this caused by the bloody onslaught of two forest kings?"

Cethern said, "Yes. A pair of light-haired warriors set upon me. Their faces were the size of wooden bowls, one larger than the other."

Cúchulainn said they could be none other than two warriors from Maeve's great household, Braen and Láréne.

Fingin asked about another wound and Cethern said he was attacked by three men, all alike. They had a bronze chain between them, deadly with spikes and spears.

"Those were the Three Scabbards of Banba, from Cúroi mac Dáire's people."

"This wound", said Fingin again, "was also caused by three warriors, I think."

Cethern said, "Yes. Three warriors set upon me with war clubs, wearing collars of silver round their necks. Each had a handful of lances. They stuck a spear in me, but I struck back with it."

Cúchulainn said, "They were the warriors from Iruath."

Fingin said, "They have cut the bloody sinews of his heart. It is rolling around inside him like a ball of wool in an empty bag."

Fingin went on to say that other wounds seemed to be the work of three more furious men.

Cethern replied, "Yes. Three grey-bellied men came at me, discussing my good points as they travelled along. They were three of Maeve and Ailill's stewards."

Fingin said, "These blows were struck early in the morning."

Cethern replied, "That's right. Three warriors attacked me, wrapped in black fur cloaks, worn bald. Their hooded tunics were covered in satin and they sported three iron cudgels in their hands."

Cúchulainn said, "They were the Three Madmen of Baische, three servants of Queen Maeve."

Fingin said, "Two warriors must have attacked here."

Cethern said, "Yes. Two great warriors with dark-green cloaks set upon me with curved scallop-edged shields. Each had a broad, grey, slender-shafted stabbing spear in his hand."

Cúchulainn said, "They were Croman of the King's Pillar and Cormac, Mael Foga's son."

Fingin remarked that their wounds came close together. They had got into his gullet.

"Two brothers struck him in this place," he said, pointing to another wound.

Cethern said, "You may be right. A pair of warriors set upon me, one with a head of yellow curls, the other with a head of dark curls. They sported two bright shields decorated with animal figures and two bright-hilted iron swords. Red-embroidered hooded tunics were wrapped about them."

Cúchulainn said he knew them.

Fingin said, pointing again, "This was a double wound from a son and a father."

Cethern said, "Yes. Two large men came at me. Their eyes were shining and they wore gold crowns on their heads. They also had gold-hilted swords at their waists. Scabbards with tassels of speckled gold hung down to their feet."

Cúchulainn said they were Ailill and his son. He asked Fingin what he thought of the matter.

Fingin said, "I will not tell a lie. His case is clear. A whole horde has left its tracks in him and his life is now about to end."

Cethern said, "Your advice is no better than the others'."

He struck him with his fist and sent him across his chariot's two shafts, smashing the chariot.

Cúchulainn said, "That was a mighty blow to deliver to an old man. Save your kicks for the enemy."

Cethern was given a choice. Either he could continue to suffer for a whole year and live out the rest of his life, or he could live for only a short while but with enough strength to fight his existing enemies. He chose the second option.

Cúchulainn made a mash out of bones, and Cethern slept in the marrow. He had no ribs left, so Cúchulainn fashioned a ribcage out of the chariot frame.

Then Cethern said, "If only I had my own weapons, I would do deeds that people would talk about for ever."

Cúchulainn said he thought he saw Fin Bec coming towards them in a chariot. Eochaid's daughter was Fin's wife, and she was with him. They had brought Cethern's weapons in their chariot.

Cethern took his weapons and made off towards the armies, with the frame of his chariot bound around his belly to give him strength.

The healer Itholl, who had pretended to be dead amongst the bodies of the other healers, warned the Connaught camp. In their fear they placed Ailill's crown on top of a pillar-stone.

Cethern attacked it and drove his sword through it, and his fist after the sword. This stone was named Lia Toll ('the pierced stone') and it is in Crích Rois.

Cethern cried, "You have played me false. Someone must put on this crown of Ailill's and come out to fight with me."

Eventually one of them placed the crown on his head and attacked him in his chariot. Cethern threw his shield at him and it split him and the charioteer open. It cleaved the horses and drove them into the ground. The enemy then came in force, and Cethern wrought havoc amongst them until he fell.

Fintan came to avenge his son Cethern with 150 belted warriors, all with double-headed spears. They fought seven battles and only Fintan and his son Crimthann escaped alive. All their followers died. Crimthann became separated from his father by a wall of shields and was saved by Ailill on condition that he would fight them no more until he came with Conchobor to the last battle. Fintan promised that he would be Ailill's friend, and Ailill gave him back his son.

Menn mac Sálchada attacked the men of Erin with thirty men, and twelve of Maeve's men fell as well as twelve of his own. Menn himself was badly wounded, and all his followers were reddened with blood. The men of Erin said it was a shame for Menn, for his people were killed and ruined, and he himself was wounded and covered in blood. Menn left the encampment, and no further warriors were killed. He returned to his home in the lands around the Boann river, and he stayed there until he was to come with Conchobor to the last battle. It was not considered a dishonour for him to do this.

Cúchulainn commanded his charioteer to try to get help from Rochad mac Faithemaib. The charioteer came across him and asked him to come and help Cúchulainn if he had recovered from his pangs. Rochad came south with 100 warriors.

Ailill was scanning the plain when he saw a troop crossing it, and he asked Fergus who it was. Fergus replied that it was Rochad mac Faithemaib coming to help Cúchulainn.

Ailill said, "Send out 100 warriors into the middle of the plain with Finnabair in front of them. Send a horseman to tell Rochad that the girl wants to speak to him alone. If we can get our hands upon him, it will prevent him from harming our army."

It happened that Finnabair loved Rochad, for he was the handsomest warrior in Ulster at that time. She went to Maeve and told her that she had loved this warrior for some time. He was her first love.

Maeve said, "If you have so much love for him, sleep with him tonight and ask him for a truce until he comes against us with Conchobor on the day of the great battle."

The horseman delivered the message from Finnabair, and Rochad went alone to talk with her. Her troop rushed at him from all sides and grasped him in their arms. In such a manner he was captured. His followers fled. He was set free when he promised not to fight the armies until he came with Conchobor to the last battle. He was offered Finnabair in exchange for his promise, and the girl slept with him.

The seven kings of Munster were told that Rochad had slept with Finnabair, and one of them said that the girl had already been promised to him to get him to join the army. Fifteen hostages had been given as a guarantee. All seven confessed in turn that she had been promised to them. They went to wreak vengeance against Ailill's sons, who were keeping watch over the armies in Glen Domain, but Maeve attacked them. The Galeóin troop of 3,000 also rose up, as did Ailill and Fergus. Several hundred died in this fight.

When Finnabair heard this had happened because of her, she fell dead of shame. This event gave the place its name – Finnabair Slébe ('Finnabair in the mountains').

Now Ilech attacked them at Ath Feidli. Ilech was Laegaire Buadach's grandfather, and the father of Connad the Yellow-Haired, Ilech's son. Ilech came to take vengeance upon the army in an old chariot without covers or cushions. Two old yellow horses pulled the ancient chariot. The whole frame was filled with stones and clods that he flung at anyone who came to look at him in his nakedness. The army kept jeering at the naked man, but Dóchae mac Mágach stopped the rabble. He called out to Ilech that he would take his sword and his head that day if he did not get out of the army's way.

Ilech saw the mash of marrow, and they told him that it was made out of Ulster's cow bones. On the same day he made another marrow mash out of Connaught men's bones. As night fell Dóchae cut off Ilech's head and brought it to Ilech's grandson Laegaire. He made a pact of friendship with Laegaire and kept his sword.

The armies moved towards Tailtiu, where 150 Ulster warriors killed three times their own number, but they themselves met their death. The place is named Roi Arad ('the battlefield of the charioteer'), for a charioteer and his company fell there on the Táin Bó Cúailnge.

The armies saw one evening a great stone hurtling towards them from the east, and another like it from the west. The two stones met in the air and fell over the camp of Fergus and Ailill. This sport continued until the same time the next day, while the armies sat still with their shields held over their heads to guard against falling blocks of stone. The plain grew full of stones. This is the origin of the name Stony Plain. Cúroi mac Dáire was the cause. He had come to help his own people, and he stopped at Cotail.

Munremur mac Gerrcind arrived from Emain Macha to assist Cúchulainn. Cúroi knew there was no one in the armies that could confront Munremur. Munremur and Cúroi made a pact: Cúroi went back to his home and Munremur went to Emain Macha. Munremur did not come back again until the day of the last battle.

While these things were happening the pangs of the Ulstermen were wearing off. From Raíth Sualdam, his house on the plain of Murtheimne, Sualdam heard how his son Cúchulainn was being troubled.

He said, "Have the heavens rent? Is the sea bursting its bounds? Is the end of the world near? Or is it that my son is crying out as he fights against tremendous odds?"

He went out to his son, but Cúchulainn did not want him there. He said that if anyone killed Sualdam, he would not have the strength to avenge him. Cúchulainn told him to go to the men of

Ulster and ask them to come and fight with him. If they did not come soon, they would never get their revenge.

His father could see that there was no part of Cúchulainn's body bigger than the tip of a rush that had not been pierced. In his left hand alone, despite the fact that it protected him, there were fifty bloody places.

Sualdam travelled to Emain Macha, and cried out to the men of Ulster that warriors had been murdered, women stolen and cattle plundered. He gave his first cry from the slope of the enclosure, his second beside the fort and his third from the Mound of the Hostages within Emain Macha itself. There was no answer. In Ulster no man spoke – not even Cúchulainn or Conchobor – before the Druids.

Sualdam said, "Our people are harassed as far as Dún Sobairche and the cattle and women have been taken. Cúchulainn has kept the men of Erin out of Murtheimne Plain and Crích Rois. For three winters he has fastened his cloak around him with hoops of twigs and kept dry wisps in his joints. He was wounded to such an extent that his joints were coming asunder."

The Druid said that by right he should suffer death, and Conchobor said it would be fitting, but the men of Ulster cried out.

It appeared to Sualdam that they were not doing enough and he ran out whilst they were talking. He fell over his shield and the edge of it cut his head off. His head was brought back on the shield to his house at Emain Macha, where it uttered the same warning again.

Conchobor said, "What is all the uproar? Have we not still got the sea before us, the sky above us, the earth under our feet? We shall beat them in battle and bring back every cow to its byre. Every woman and child will be brought back home."

Conchobor laid his hands upon his son, Finnchad Fer Benn ('the horned man'), so called because of the silver horns he sported.

He said, "Rise up, Finnchad, and summon Deda to me from his bay, along with Leaman and Flach and Fergus's son Illann from Gabar."

Many others were summoned too.

Finnchad discovered that this task was easy, for all the chieftains in Conchobor's province had been waiting for the order to move. They had gathered round Emain Macha from the east, as well as the north and west, and they entered Emain Macha in time for Conchobor's awakening. They moved out of the fort southward to seek out the armies of Erin.

The first stage of their march was from Emain Macha to Iraird Cuillenn. Conchobor asked why they were stopping here. They said they had gone with thirty warriors to Temair to get Erc son of Coirpre Niafer and Fedelm Noichride. They said they would not move until their two troops and 3,000 warriors arrived.

Conchobor said he could not wait until the men of Erin discovered he had recovered from his wounds, so he and Celtchar travelled ahead with 150 chariots. They returned with eight score men's heads from Airthir Midi Ford, in East Meath. The ford is now known as Ath Féne ('the warriors' ford'). They had eight score women with them, as well as their share of the plunder.

When Conchobor and Celtchar brought the heads back to the camp, ground was given up to four horse chariots, and there were 200 Druids to lead them. There was a man not lacking at Conchobor's back.

The cry went up: "Prepare for battle! Let the warriors awake!"

The battle started at Gáirech and Irgarech. Many think it was Conchobor's son who chanted the night before the battle, just after Laegaire Buadach had started the chant. He cried out for the kings to rise up at Emain Macha. He also chanted in the eastern camp.

During the night Dubthach Dael of Ulster dreamed about the armies, and he spoke in his sleep: "Fearful morning, fearful season; armies in turmoil, kings cast down; necks broken and three armies crushed by the hosts of Ulster. With women Conchobor will struggle, herds will be driven, heroes felled, hounds cut down, horses mangled, tunics torn. The earth will drink the spilt blood of many hordes."

Nemain brought confusion amongst the armies and 100 of them fell dead. Silence prevailed again until Cormac (some say Ailill mac Mata) was heard chanting in the western camp. He cried out that it was Ailill's hour; there would be a great truce (the truce of Cuillenn) and a great plot (the plot at Delind); great were the hordes of horses, the herds at Assal; there would be a great plague at Tuath Bressi.

Chapter 18

The Armies March

During this time, the Connaught army took counsel with Ailill, Maeve and Fergus. They proposed to send scouts to see if the men of Ulster had reached the plain. Aillil sent Mac Roth to go and see if they were already on the plain of Meath.

"If they are not yet there," he said, "we can get clear away with their belongings. They can look for a fight as much as they want now, but I am not waiting any longer for them."

Mac Roth scanned the plain, and reported back to Ailill, Maeve and Fergus. When he first looked out from the Sliab Fuait road he had seen all the wild animals leaving the forests and coming over the plain. When he looked a second time, he had seen a great fog filling the valleys and hollows, so that the high places in between appeared as islands in a lake. Sparks of fire could be seen through the dense fog, as well as a riot of different colours. There were flashes of lightning, with much thunder. Though there had been only a breeze, a great wind blew up and flung him down on his back. It all but swept the hair from his head. Fergus told Ailill he knew well what this meant: the men of Ulster had risen from their pangs. They had entered the forest, great warriors thronging in might and violence. They had sent the wild animals fleeing on to the plain. The lightning and the sparks of fire were in the warriors' eyes. The thunder and turmoil was the clashing of their blades and their ivory-hilted swords, the noise of chariots, horses' hoofs hammering, the anger and ferocity of the brave warriors as they went into battle.

Fergus said he had warriors to meet them. But there was no one in the western world, from Greece to the Orkney Islands and the Pillars of Hercules, who could withstand the men of Ulster when their fury was aroused.

Mac Roth set off again to see if the men were coming. He set out for their encampment on the smooth plain of Slemain Midi.

When he returned he gave Maeve, Ailill and Fergus this news: "A mighty force is coming to Slemain Midi. It is a full troop of 3,000. They tore off their clothes and built a mound of sods where their leader was to sit. He is fair, graceful and tall – a royal figure before his company. He is handsome and slender. He has light-yellow hair curled neatly and reaching down to his shoulders. He was dressed in a purple pleated tunic. A brooch of red-gold fastened the cloak at his breast. His eyes are grey and gentle, his face shining, his brow broad, his jaw narrow. He has a beard. He carried a gold-hilted sword and a shield graven with gold animals. In his hand he held the slender shaft of a broad grey stabbing spear. He is the finest of the world's princes in figure and dress. He advanced with great dignity."

Mac Roth said that another company was coming, second only to the first in numbers and discipline, dress and fierceness.

"A young warrior headed the company. A green cloak was wrapped around him, fastened at his shoulder with a green brooch. His hair is yellow and curled. He wore at his left an ivory-hilted sword, the hilt cut from a boar's tusk. A bordered tunic covered him to his knees. He carried a scallop-edged, death-dealing shield and a great spear with silver rings running along the shaft as far as the tip. This company had settled down at the left hand of the first company. They squatted down with their knees upon the earth and their shields at their chins. I heard a stammer in the speech of the great champion who led that company."

Mac Roth said that another company was coming, and it looked like a host of 3,000.

"A wild man went before them. He had brown curly hair and a long, thin forked beard. He wore a dark-grey fringed cloak, fastened at his breast by a leaf-shaped pin of gold. A white hooded tunic covered him to his knees, and he carried a hero's shield decorated with animals. A naked sword with a bright silver grip hung at his waist and a spear was in his hand. He sat down, facing the leader of the first company."

Ailill asked Fergus who they were.

Fergus replied, "I know the companies well. Conchobor is the one on the mound of sods. Sencha mac Ailella, the most eloquent man in Ulster, is the one that sat facing him. Cúscraid Menn Macha, the stammerer, Conchobor's son, sat by his father's side. The spear in his hand always plays like that on the eve of a victory. I swear by my people's gods that no army raised in Erin could ever resist the men of Ulster."

Mac Roth said that another company came, a troop of about 3,000 with a bold champion at its head.

"He is awesome and terrible. His dark brown hair lies flat on his forehead. He carried a curved shield and a five-pronged spear in his hands, and a forked javelin hung at his side. A sword was slung behind him. He was wrapped about with a purple cloak with a gold brooch at his shoulder, and a white-hooded tunic covered him to his knees."

Ailill asked Fergus who it was, and Fergus replied, "It is a beginner in battle, but a man made for war. He will fall upon his enemies like doom."

Another great dreadful company arrived at the hill at Slemain Midi, Mac Roth reported, with their cloaks thrown back behind them. They brought great terror with them. The clash of the great warriors was great as they marched.

"A fearsome champion is their leader. He has grey hair and large yellow eyes. He was wrapped in a yellow cloak with a white border. A great shield hung at his side, and he carried a javelin and a long spear with a blood-stained shaft. Next to the shield was another javelin, with the blood of enemies on its blade. A large, murderous sword hung at his shoulders."

Ailill asked who it was, and Fergus replied, "It is a warrior that has never shirked the warlike fray. It is Laegaire Buadach ('the victorious'), son of Connad, son of Ilech from Impail in the north."

Another large host was coming to the hill at Slemain Midi, Mac Roth reported.

"A pleasant, fat, thick-necked warrior was at their head. His hair is black and curled. His face was flushed, and his grey eyes were shining. He wore a brown cloak held by a bright silver brooch. He carried a bright shield with a knob of bronze, and a spear was in his hand. He was covered in a red-embroidered braided tunic, and an ivory-hilted sword hung over his clothes.

Ailill asked Fergus who it was, and he said, "It is a man who will fall upon his enemies like a bitter doom."

Another large company was coming to the hill of Slemain Midi, fine and handsome, well dressed and disciplined, Mac Roth said.

"They hurried to the hill, and they alarmed the armies with the noise of their weapons as they advanced. A proud champion came to their head – the most impressive among men for his hair and eyes and countenance, for apparel, bearing, voice and proud looks, for weapons, skill and style, for equipment, great feats, learning, distinction and breeding."

Fergus said, "It is the bright flame of the fair Fedlimid coming in a warrior's rage with irresistible might, full of triumph from the destruction of his enemies in other lands."

Another host was coming to the hill at Slemain Midi, Mac Roth said – full warlike troops of 3,000 at the last count.

"A great warrior stood bravely at their head. His hair is black and curly, his eyes full of rage. He wore a grey cloak held at the shoulder with a silver pin, and a white hooded tunic. He carried a sword and a red shield with a knob of tough silver. He held a broad blade in his hand."

Ailill asked who it was, and Fergus said, "It is Connad mac Morna, coming from Callann with an angry face. He is bold in battle, a winner of wars."

Another company was coming to the hill at Slemain Midi, Mac Roth said – a large host.

"Seldom would be found a champion of better style and bearing than the leader at the head of this company. His red-gold hair is close-cropped, his face is well formed, his jaw is narrow, his brow is broad, and he has fine red lips and shining teeth. His voice is clear. He is the most marvellous of men. He wore a purple cloak wrapped around him with a great brooch on his white breast. He carried a curved shield with a knob of silver, graven with all sorts of animals. He held a javelin and a lean spear. A gold sword with a gold hilt hung at his back. He wore a red embroidered tunic wrapped around him."

Ailill asked who it was, and Fergus said, "I know him well. He is formidable."

Another company was coming to the hill of Slemain Midi, Mac Roth said, with a great hero at their head.

"His legs and arms are as thick as a man. From head to foot he is a man to be reckoned with. The style of his warriors made a great spectacle as he came amongst them in triumph – a hero full of dignity. Steadily they advanced on Slemain Midi."

Fergus said, "This man is a flood of hot blood, power and pride – forced to hold armies together."

Another great host was coming to the hill at Slemain Midi, Mac Roth said, dressed in weird clothes, bringing strife before them, with a fine hero at their head.

"He is magnificent in all aspects – his hair and eyes, his stature, structure and ferocity. He was dressed in five chains of gold, a white hooded tunic and a green cloak fastened at the shoulder with a gold brooch. He held a great spear in his hand, and a gold-hilted sword hung by his shoulder."

Fergus said, "He is a hungry hero, quicker at temper. It is Amargin, the son of smith Ecit Salach ('the grim one'), and he comes from the north."

Another company was coming to the hill at Slemain Midi, Mac Roth said, overwhelming in numbers, full of strength, and making a noise like thunder.

"A terrible hero led the company with harsh looks. He is big-bellied, big-nosed and thick-lipped. His hair is tough and grizzled. His limbs are red. He wore a rough tunic and a dark cloak with an iron spike fastening the cloak. He carried a curved shield and a large javelin in his hand, with thirty rivets. A sword that has been used seven times hung at his shoulders, and the entire army rose up to greet him. Troop after troop of them fell into disorder as he marched upon the hill."

Fergus said, "He fights fiercely, like an ocean wave breaking over barriers."

Another company was coming to the hill at Slemain Midi, Mac Roth said.

"At its head was a warrior all in white. He sported a shield with a knob of gold in his hand, and he carried a broad stabbing spear. He advanced into battle like a great hero."

Fergus said, "He is a most cherished, powerful and death-healing warrior, murderous as a bear to the enemy. He is the fair and righteous Feradach Finn Fechtnach and he comes from the wood at Sliab Fuait in the north."

Another company was coming to the hill at Slemain Midi, Mac Roth said.

"A fierce warrior was out in front. He has a large belly and thick lips, his hair is dark and curly and he has only one eye. His head is rough and his hand is long. He wore a black cloak, fastened with a disc of tin. He carried a grey shield at his left, a boar-stabbing spear, banded at the neck, was in his right hand, and a long sword hung at his shoulders."

Fergus said, "He is sharp and busy in battle, not to be withstood as he rages upon the earth. He is Errge Echbél ('the horse-lipped') and he comes from Brí Errgi in the north."

Yet another company was coming to the hill at Slemain Midi, Mac Roth said.

"Two heroes were at their head, alike in looks. They have heads of yellow hair. They carried bright graven shields of silver animals, and they are the same age."

"Two heroes, two pure flames, two battle-spikes!" said Fergus. "Two champions and pillars of the fray! Two fires, two warrior battle champions!"

Ailill asked Fergus who they were, and he said, "They are Fiachna and Fiacha, the two sons of Conchobor mac Nesa, the darling of the north of Ireland."

Another company was coming to the hill of Slemain Midi, Mac Roth said.

"Three noble and fierce champions were at their head, with flushed faces. All three had cropped hair of gold-yellow. Cloaks of a similar colour were wrapped about them, fastened at their shoulders with gold pins. They sported red-embroidered tunics and they all carried similar shields. Gold-hilted swords hung at their shoulders and they carried broad spears in their hands. All three are of a similar age."

Fergus said, "They are three fiery torches from Cuib and Midluachair. They have done great deeds. They are princes, hardened soldiers from east of Sliab Fuait. They are Fiachna's three sons, and they have come to recover the bull."

Yet another company was coming to the hill at Slemain Midi, Mac Roth pointed out.

"There is a lively man at its head, with hot-looking eyes. He is a hero. He wore a speckled cloak held with a silver disc. He carried a grey shield in his left hand and a silver-hilted sword hung by his side. He held in his right hand a javelin shaped well for battle. A white hooded tunic covered him to the knees. The soldiers about him were red with blood, and he himself was marked with it."

Fergus said, "This is a piteous situation. In battle he is like a gashing beast, a wild boar, a raving bull. He is the conqueror from Baile, the defender of the gap, the protector of the border of the north of Ireland. He is Menn mac Sálchada. He has come from Corann to avenge his wounds."

Another company was coming to the hill at Slemain Midi, Mac Roth said.

"It was spirited and eager and a formidable warrior was at its head. He has dark curling hair and wore a fine woollen cloak and a handsome tunic. A gold pin held the cloak at his shoulder. A sword hung at his left side – a great beauty with a hilt of bright silver. He also carried a red shield and a grey stabbing spear, beautifully manufactured and set into its shaft of ash."

Fergus said, "This warrior is a man of three hard strokes, a man of three roads and highways and byways, a man of three qualities and three cries. He breaks enemies in battle."

Another host was coming to the hill at Slemain Midi, Mac Roth said, and it looked like a troop of 3,000 warriors.

"Their leader was dressed mostly in white, and he competed with Ailill in appearance. He wore a crown and a red tunic. A magnificent cloak was wrapped around him, fastened at the breast with a gold brooch. He carried a gold-rimmed, deadly shield and a spear, and a gold-hilted sword hung at his shoulder."

Fergus said, "Like the sea against a stream he comes – a great blaze of fury against his foes."

Yet another company was coming to the hill at Slemain Midi, Mac Roth said, in numbers not like other companies. Their clothes were remarkable and the company was a great army in itself.

"A freckled boy was at its head – the handsomest of boys. He carried on his arm a gold-rimmed shield with a white knob, and a light javelin shimmered in his hand. He wore a white, red-embroidered, white-hooded tunic and a purple fringed cloak was wrapped around him, held at the breast with a silver pin. A great sword hung over his clothes."

At that, Fergus was silent. He did not know anyone like that boy in Ulster.

At last he said, "These may be the men of Temair gathered about the fine and noble Erc, son of Coirpre Niafer and Conchobor's daughter. Coirpre and Conchobor are not friendly with each other, and the boy may have travelled to help his grandfather without requesting his father's leave. I am afraid you, Ailill, will lose the battle on account of this boy. He knows no fear or terror. When he presses into the midst of your forces the fighting men of Ulster will raise a great shout and fight furiously to save the little calf of their hearts. If they see the boy in terrible straits, they will suddenly get into a great rage and hack a path through the battle. Conchobor's sword will be heard like a mastiff growling as he comes to save the boy. Conchobor will throw up three mounds of men around the battlefield in the search for his little grandson. Full of family spirit, the fighting men of Ulster will fall on their enemies."

Mac Roth said he was tired of describing what he had seen, but there was something more to be said.

"Conall Cernach and his great force has not yet come. Conchobor's three sons and their three troops of 3,000 warriors have also not yet come. Cúchulainn, wounded in his struggle, also has not yet come. Many hundreds and thousands have reached the Ulster camp. Many heroes and champions and warriors have hurried to the gathering, but more companies are on their way. My eyes travelled from Ferdia's ford to Slemain Midi and fell upon men and horses instead of hills and slopes.

Chapter 19

The Last Battle

Conchobor arrived with his forces and spoke to Ailill about a truce until sunrise. Ailill consented for the men of Erin and the exiles, and Conchobor agreed for the men of Ulster. Conchobor's tents were pitched and he settled in his camp surrounded by his followers. The men of Ulster had settled before sunset, and the ground between the two forces lay bare.

In the twilight, the Morrígan chanted: "Ravens eating at men's necks, blood spurting in the fierce fray, hacked flesh, battle madness, blades in bodies, acts of war, after the cloak made in man's shape to be hacked to pieces, the men of Cruachan with strong blows, war was waged, each trampling upon the other. Hail Ulster! Woe men of Ireland! Woe to Ulster! Hail men of Ireland!"

The last "Woe to Ulster!" she said in Connaught men's ears, in order to hide the truth from them. On the same night Net's wives called out to the men of Erin near the field of Gáirech and Irgarech, and 100 warriors died of fright. It was a bad night for them.

Ailill mac Mata chanted on the eve of the battle, saying, "Rise up, Traigthrén, swift-footed!"

He was to summon for them many warriors.

All these men, in groups of three, were the men of Erin that had survived the slaughter of Cúchulainn.

At this time Cúchulainn was lying nearby at Fedan Chollnaan.

People visited him each day and brought him food. West of Ferdia's ford he had killed no one. Cúchulainn was told that a small herd of animals had strayed from the western camp and that some servants were coming out after them to bring them back. Cúchulainn said, "The servants will start to fight and the animals will wander over the plain."

Everyone went to help the servants.

Cúchulainn asked how the Ulstermen were fighting, and Laeg replied, "Like true men. Their honour will make them die for the sake of the herds. Beardless boys have joined the fight."

Cúchulainn enquired whether the light of the sun had touched the clouds yet, and Laeg replied, "Not yet."

Cúchulainn said, "If only I had the strength to join them!"

The charioteer said, "There will be enough slaughter today without that."

At sunrise, the better-born folk were ready for battle, but the kings had not come yet. They were still asleep.

Fachtna (some say Conchobor) chanted in his sleep: "Rise, kings of Macha, modest people of mighty acts. Blades are battering, battle is raging, the earth is torn up, shields are beaten, arms are weary, and herds are bellowing in the fight. Battle ranks are trampled underfoot, lords and princes lead in battle. A forest of men marches and falls. Blood is strained. Hearts of queens are filled with grief. Rise, kings of Emain Macha!"

The sentries were on the alert.

Laegaire Buadach said, "Rise, kings of Macha, guard your cattle, guard your plunder, drive the Connaught armies from Uisnech Hill. Men's flanks are in danger, sinews are on fire. I shall conquer the world on the field of Gáirech."

"Wait a while longer," Conchobor said, "until the hills are lit with the men of Erin."

Then Cúchulainn, from the east, watched Connaught kings setting their crowns upon their heads and coming to lead the companies. He told Laeg to rouse the men of Ulster.

Laeg spoke, though some say it was the poet Amargin mac Ecit: "Rise up, kings of Macha, modest people of mighty deeds.

The cattle of Impail with the heart's gore was poured out. Strife filled men's veins in order to feed brave acts. But the battle din was dying, and was there anyone but Cúchulainn to carry out Macha's will for Cúailnge's cattle? Rise early now!"

The charioteer cried out that he had aroused them and that they were rushing naked into battle with nothing but their weapons. Those that faced the east dashed out through the backs of their tents!

Cúchulainn said, "Necessity is a great spur. Friend Laeg, how are the men of Ulster performing in battle?"

Laeg said, "Like true men. They are fighting closely. There is no place for even a chariot's wheel rim to pass through."

Cúchulainn said, "It has the makings of a great battle. Inform me of events – leave nothing out."

Laeg said he would try his best.

The warriors from the west had reached the battle line in the east and had broken through. The same number from the west had reached the eastern battle line.

Cúchulainn exclaimed, "Alas! You would see me attacking there with the rest of them if I had my health."

The men of Erin, in groups of three, advanced to the ford. It was a great spectacle as they marched to the field of Gáirech and Irgarech. The nine charioteers from Iruath advanced with them. Three men were on foot out in front, as swift as those in the chariots. But Queen Maeve now held them back from battle, in order to pluck Ailill from the fray if their armies were defeated or to kill Conchobor.

Laeg told Cúchulainn that Ailill and Maeve were asking Fergus to join in the fight, reproaching him with all they had done for him during his exile.

"If only I had my sword," Fergus said, "for I would send men's severed heads toppling down like hailstones over their shields into the mud. It would be like a king's horse churning up the ground. I swear by my people's gods", he said, "I would heap up men's hacked jawbones on men's necks, and on men's shoulders. Their arms would be on their elbows."

139

Ailill asked his charioteer to bring him his flesh-piercing sword. Then Ailill said, "Take this sword and lay Ireland low, but spare us at Gáirech, mighty man amongst boys."

Fergus said to Ailill that it would be unfortunate if he fell on this field of battle, but he seized his weapon and proceeded into the fray. With his sword held in two hands, he carved a gap of about 100 men in the ranks – 100 warriors died by his sword on the first attack. Then he came on Conall Cernach.

Conall said, "You fight hard against your own kith and kin for the sake of a whore's backside."

Maeve lifted her weapons and hurried into battle. Three times she drove all before her until she was turned back by a flight of javelins.

Conchobor noticed that someone was forcing the battle against them from the north, but his warriors said that they would hold out until the earth gave under them, or until the heavens fell on them and forced them to give way.

Conchobor sought out Fergus and raised his shield against him – the Shield of the Ear of Beauty, with its four gold horns and four coverings of gold. Fergus struck it three times, but he could not budge the rim of the shield enough to reach Conchobor's head.

Fergus said, "What man of Ulster holds this shield?"

Conchobor replied, "A better man than you. One who drove you out into exile with the wild dogs and foxes. I shall stop your battle-deeds today before all the men of Erin."

Fergus raised his sword against Conchobor, but Cormac Connlongas flung his arms about him and caught his two wrists.

"Be careful! Be careful, friend Fergus," Cormac said. "You do not want to spoil friendships. The blows will cheapen your enmity and break pacts."

Fergus cried, "Where should I attack?"

He was told, "Turn your head aside and strike out crosswise at those three hills. Remember that Ulster's honour was never given away and never will be." Then Cormac said to Conchobor, "This man will vent his rage on Ulstermen no more."

At this, Fergus turned aside and struck at the hills, and with three strokes he levelled the three hills of Meath. Cúchulainn heard the blows that Fergus dealt at the hills, and at Conchobor's shield.

He said, "Who struck the blows in the distance? Blood blocks his heart and battle-madness prevails. Fergus mac Róich in mounting glory has struck at them."

Laeg answered, "Fergus mac Róich has a sword hidden in the chariot shaft."

Cúchulainn said, "Loosen the hazel twigs quickly. Men are being covered in blood, and bodies are being swallowed up."

The rushes sprang up like larks, and the bindings of hazel twigs soared away from him as far as Mag Tuag ('the plain of the hazel bands') in Connaught.

Cúchulainn ran about confused, and his wounds opened up again.

Maeve had sent two handmaids to care for him and make his wounds open afresh, telling him how Fergus had fallen and Ulster had been defeated in battle while he was kept from the fight.

He smashed their heads together so that each was coloured grey with the other's brains. The war-spasm seized him, and they put twenty-seven skin tunics around him, which he wore into battle. He took his whole chariot on his back – the entire frame and the two rimmed wheels. He rushed forward into battle and he circled around looking for Fergus.

Cúchulainn cried out three times before Fergus answered. He swore by Ulster's gods to churn him like foam in a pool. He would stand over him like a cat's tail erect. He would batter him as easily as a woman cares for her son.

Cúchulainn said the son of Sualdam and Conchobor's sister had given way before him. Fergus said he promised to do that, and Cúchulainn said the time had come.

"Very well," said Fergus.

Fergus went off with his troop of 3,000, and the men of Galeóin and the men of Munster went away as well. They left Ailill and

Maeve to the battle with their seven sons and troops of 3,000 warriors.

When Cúchulainn joined the battle it was noon. The sun shone down on the trees when he defeated their last company, and nothing was left of his chariot but a handful of ribs out of the frame and a handful of spokes from the wheel.

Maeve had set up a shelter of shields to guard the rear of the men of Erin. She had sent off the brown bull of Cúailnge, and it was taken safely away, as she had promised. Now Queen Maeve got her gush of blood.

"Fergus," she said, "take over the shelter of the shields at the rear of the men of Erin."

They dug three great channels, each big enough to house a family, and the place has been called Fual Medba ('Maeve's place') ever since.

Cúchulainn found her, but he held his hand. He would not strike her from behind. Maeve asked him to spare her, and Cúchulainn said if he killed her it would only be right. But he did spare her. He was not a killer of women.

He watched until they passed Ath Luain, and there he stopped. He struck three blows of his sword at the stone hills nearby (the Bald-Topped Hills, as they are known today), and now the battle was over.

Maeve said to Fergus that they had experienced great shame that day.

Fergus said, "We followed the will of a misguided woman. It is the usual practice for a herd led by a mare to be slaughtered."

They took the bull away the day after the battle. On Ai Plain, at Tarbga, he met the bull Finnbennach ('the white horned'). Everyone stopped what they were doing, in order to see the two bulls fighting. The men of Ireland asked who should be the judge, and they agreed that it should be Bricriu mac Carbad.

The two bulls careered across him and killed him. The brown bull of Cúailnge planted a hoof on the other bull's horn, and all day until nightfall he would not bring the hoof back. Fergus criticized it and took a stick to its flank. Fergus said it would look bad if it threw away its reputation. Men had died on both sides because of it.

The bull jerked back its hoof and its leg broke, but the other bull's horn was sent flying to a nearby mountain, called the Mountain of the Horn to this day.

Night fell upon the men of Erin. They could hear the uproar in the darkness. At night the bulls circled the whole of Ireland.

When daybreak came the men of Erin saw the brown bull coming westwards past Cruachan with the mangled remains of Finnbennach hanging from its horns.

At nightfall it entered the lake near Cruachan and it came out with Finnbennach's loins, shoulder blades and liver on its horns. The armies decided to kill it, but Fergus intervened and let it go anywhere it liked. It headed towards its own land, and it stopped to drink at Finnlethe on the way. Finnbennach's shoulder blade was left there, named the White One's Shoulder Blade. It drank again and left Finnbennach's loins at a place now known as the Ford of the Loins. Its bellow was heard through the entire province.

Again it drank at Tromma, where Finnbennach's liver fell from its two horns, from which derives the name Tromma ('liver').

It arrived at Etan Tairb and set its course for the hill at Ath Da Ferta, from which comes the name Etan Tairb ('the bull's brow') in Murtheimne Plain.

Then it travelled the road to Cuib, where it had lived with the milk-less cow Dáire. It tore up the ground there, from which comes the name Field of the Trench.

It carried on until it fell dead between Ulster and Uí Echach at Druim Tairb ('the ridge of the bull').

Ailill and Maeve made peace with Ulster and with Cúchulainn, and for seven years afterwards none of their folk were killed in Ireland. Finnabair remained with Cúchulainn, and the Connaught men returned to their own kingdom. The men of Ulster went back to Emain Macha in triumphal procession.

Select Bibliography

Caitlin Matthews: *The Celtic Spirit* (Hodder and Stoughton, 1999).

Caitlin Matthews: *The Celtic Tradition* (Element Books, 1989).

Charles Squire: *Mythology of the Celtic People* (Bracken Books, 1996).

John O'Donohue: *Spiritual Wisdom from the Celtic World* (Bantam Books, 1999).

Joseph Jacobs: *Celtic Fairy Tales* (Leopard Books, 1995).

Lady Gregory: *Gods and Knightly Men* (Colin Smythe, 1904).

Lain Zaczek: *The Book of Irish Legends* (Cico Books, 2001).

Martin Robinson: *Rediscovering the Celts* (Harper Collins, 2000).

P. W. Joyce: *Old Celtic Romances* (Folklore Society, 2000).

W. B. Yeats: *The Book of Fairy and Folk Tales of Ireland* (The Slaney Press, 1994).